6/22/94

W9-BQI-954

A13200 431359

$6.00

Performance Practices

in

BEETHOVEN'S

Piano Sonatas

AN INTRODUCTION

BY THE SAME AUTHOR

THE PIANIST'S PROBLEMS
UNDERSTANDING MUSIC
A HISTORY OF THE SONATA IDEA:
The Sonata in the Baroque Era
The Sonata in the Classic Era
The Sonata Since Beethoven

Performance Practices

in

BEETHOVEN'S

Piano Sonatas

AN INTRODUCTION

William S. Newman

THE UNIVERSITY OF NORTH CAROLINA

W · W · NORTON & COMPANY · INC ·
NEW YORK

TO

Those Interesting, Challenging,
Inquiring Students
In "Performance Practices"

(UNC MUSIC 136)

CONTENTS

ILLUSTRATIONS

Editorial Note

Short-title references in captions and footnotes appear in full in the concluding list of Chief References (p. 96); those with a hyphenated suffix, -m, designate music scores.

Where specific citations in Beethoven's sonatas are frequent they are contracted to Op./No./movement/measure(s), as in Op. 31/3/ii/6-8. Measure and measures are abbreviated to m. and mm. as necessary.

I am indebted to G. Henle Verlag of Munich for kind permission to reproduce numerous examples directly from Bertha Wallner's fine edition of the Beethoven sonatas. All forty-six examples are referenced in the Index.

W.S.N.

PART ONE

THE
NATURE
OF THE PROBLEM
AND THE SOURCES

Introducing
the
Problem

THE STUDY OF PERFORMANCE PRACTICES IS THE STUDY OF HOW TO PLAY or sing a particular piece in accordance with the styles of its time. In recent years this kind of study has attracted an ever-increasing number of musicians, both scholars and performers. In fact, it is proving to be the one most successful means of bridging what too often becomes a dichotomy of scholar and performer.

Thus far the topic of performance practices has been explored primarily in the music of Bach, especially his keyboard music, and has already led to a substantial crop of studies. A good representative of such studies is *The Interpretation of Bach's Keyboard Works* by Erwin Bodky.[1] But as we move forward in time from Bach, we find that studies in keyboard performance practices have been fewer and fewer. After Bach one main deterrent seems to have been the notion that the music was increasingly familiar and "traditional," hence should not need so much scientific exploration. An exception is the

[1] Cambridge: Harvard University Press, 1960.

13

useful book *Interpreting Mozart on the Keyboard,* by Eva and Paul Badura-Skoda.[2] (For pre-Bach works a major impediment has been the increasing difficulty of finding solid evidence in contemporary sources.) Otherwise, in spite of the veritable flood of attention scholars have been devoting to Mozart in recent years, surprisingly little has concerned performance practices.

When we come to Beethoven the dearth is particularly striking. To be sure, prior to the bicentennial of his birth in 1970, there was all too little systematic study of any aspect of his work, but especially little of performance practices. In fact, the whole 19th century has been grossly neglected in this respect. It remains to be seen whether the bicentennial, coupled with the recent opening of research floodgates into the 19th century—now that scholars feel distant enough in time— will arouse the necessary attention to Beethoven, including the many problems of performance practices, and will also expedite the new critical edition of his complete musical works, which has been proceeding at a snail's pace for nearly a decade.[3]

To get closer to the problems of performance practices in Beethoven's music it will help first to consider a few actual performance experiences. As one such experience, there was the performance of his so-called "Tempest" Sonata, Op. 31, No. 2, in D minor, that the renowned German pianist Walter Gieseking gave at a large American university shortly before his death in 1956. On the program were also some pieces by Couperin, Debussy, and Ravel, all played with Gieseking's usual penetration and exquisite sensitivity. Only the Beethoven sonata brought some negative criticism. It was played, said the critics, too delicately—too delicately both for Beethoven and for the idea of a "tempest." Others promptly countered: "Who knows how Beethoven himself really wanted this or any other work played? What actual basis, for example, is there for that 'tempest' idea? And, in any case, must there be but one way to perform such a work? Is not any great work of art capable of several different interpretations, each equally valid in its way?"

For a second actual experience, we may go back to one of Beethoven's few students, closest associates, and most trusted observers, Carl Czerny, today chiefly remembered for his etudes. Some ten or fifteen years after Beethoven's death Czerny wrote with special emphasis, "The performer of Beethoven's works (and in general those of all Classic masters) must not tolerate any alterations of the music

[2] New York: St. Martin's Press, 1962.
[3] *Beethoven Werke*. Munich: G. Henle, 1961– . No sonatas have appeared, as of 1970, but Mr. Günter Henle has kindly written me that the new edition will differ very little, chiefly in minor editorial policies, from that prepared by Bertha Wallner in 1952–53 for G. Henle-Verlag (Wallner/*Beethoven*-m) .

14

whatsoever, no additions, no omissions."[4] Yet in 1816 Czerny played in a chamber work of Beethoven in a manner that caused Beethoven to explode over violations of that very creed. As Beethoven soon apologized in a letter to Czerny, "I burst out with that remark yesterday and I was very sorry after I had done so. But you must forgive a composer who would rather have heard a work performed exactly as written, however beautifully you played it in other respects."[5] Later another close, although jealous, associate of Beethoven, Anton Schindler, amplified on this incident. He said that Czerny, in his aspirations toward the new school of virtuosity, began to elaborate in his performances, including "indiscriminate use of the pedal, the transposition in the *cantilena* sections from the first and second octaves above middle C to the third and fourth . . . , the [added] use of trills and other ornaments, and finally a metronome-like regularity."[6] How does one reconcile what Czerny preached with what he practiced?

Or, to take one more type of actual experience, how does one reconcile two very different approaches taken by Liszt to the Beethoven sonatas, as reported in two fascinating reviews by Berlioz? When Liszt played the so-called "Moonlight" Sonata, Op. 27, No. 2, in Paris in 1835, he actually played only the middle and final movements, leaving the first movement to be played by an orchestra.[7] But previously, in 1829 or 1830, according to Berlioz' recollections in 1837, Liszt had played that first movement and played it (still?) more in keeping with tastes then current:

> . . . he added trills and tremolo, rushed and slowed the pace, similarly troubled the sad calm with impassioned chords, and made the thunder rumble in this cloudless sky darkened only by the descending sun.[8]

(All this before the critic Ludwig Rellstab had yet suggested the "Moonlight" image!) But now in 1837, when Berlioz invited Liszt to play the movement once more, this time in a private group, "the noble elegy, the same that he had previously disfigured so curiously, stood out in [all] its sublime simplicity. Not one note, not one accent was added to the accents and notes [supplied] by the composer."[9]

[4] Translated from Badura-Skoda/*Czerny*, 26 (as in Czerny's Op. 500/IV; regarding the uncertain date see Newman/*Beethoven*, 180).
[5] February 12, 1816; as translated in Anderson/*Beethoven*, II, 560.
[6] Schindler & MacArdle/*Beethoven*, 415–16; cf. 447.
[7] Prod'homme/*Beethoven*, 125–26 (citing Berlioz in the *Journal des Débats* for April 25, 1835); *Revue musicale*, XV (1835), 116.
[8] Translated from Prod'homme/*Beethoven*, 126–27 (citing Berlioz in the *Journal des Débats* for March 12, 1837).
[9] As in the previous footnote.

Furthermore, read what Berlioz also had to say after Liszt introduced the "Hammerklavier" Sonata, Op. 106, in B♭, in Paris in 1836:

> Not one note was left out, not one note was added (I followed the score closely), not one change was made in the tempo that was not indicated in the editing, not one inflection, not one idea was sacrificed or diverted from its true sense. Above all in the *Adagio*—in the performance of this wondrous hymn that the spirit of Beethoven seems to have sung by itself while soaring alone in the immensity—he [Liszt] steadfastly kept up with the level of the composer's thought. . . .[10]

These three real-life experiences concern not only a variety of performance problems proper. They also raise questions as to the limits of artistic propriety, and they concern different time intervals in relation to the composer. Regarding the time intervals, it is interesting that Czerny's interpretations while the composer was still very much alive and Liszt's only shortly after his death were already straying considerably further from the authentic score than Gieseking ever strayed in all his concertizing a century and a quarter later. Obviously what is needed is, first of all, better information about such performance problems than we have had up to now. Then may follow better interpretations of the available information, and, finally, the necessary tempering of both information and interpretations with sufficient historical perspective.

Consuming curiosity about such problems, from the standpoints of performer, teacher, and writer alike, has been the author's long-time motivation for the present, introductory book. But a more recent and pressing impetus came from participation in a faculty foursome that presented the complete "thirty-two" in eight monthly recitals,[11] generating intense fruitful discussions, among the participants and others, of particular performance questions. Along with several concentrated, specialized studies (cited later where they apply), one result has been this more general book, whose over-all plan has turned out to be twofold: 1) a brief summary of the whole problem of performance practices in Beethoven's piano sonatas, as well as of the pertinent sources; and 2) eight sample probings into eight different but specific aspects of the problem. One should hardly need to emphasize that the description "brief summary" does apply here, for almost any one of the topics

[10] Translated from Prod'homme/*Beethoven*, 248–49 (citing Berlioz in the *Revue et Gazette musicale*, June 12, 1836, p. 200); but there no longer seems to be any need to confirm that the sonata in question was indeed Op. 106.
[11] At The University of North Carolina, 1967–68, and on the university television station, 1968–69.

introduced could readily be expanded into a book-length study of its own. In the remainder of this introduction-to-the-introduction, a bit of orientation (or reorientation) is offered for those who require it.

Beethoven was born in Bonn in 1770, moved to Vienna in 1792, and remained in that center until he died in 1827. Although he lived well into the early Romantic era, he stemmed directly from the great Classic masters Haydn and Mozart. But in his eminence and his hermitic deafness Beethoven is usually placed by historians on a Parnassus of his own. Compared with the nine symphonies, a few vocal works, six concertos, seventeen string quartets, and other compositions, his "thirty-two" (and still other solo piano sonatas) give the broadest and most representative view of his output, both because he himself attached so much importance to them and because he continued to write them throughout most of his creative years.[12] A chart of these sonatas is inserted on pp. 18–19 for subsequent reference. It includes the opus numbers; the keys; the original or most used names for some of them; where the autograph is, if extant; where and when any complete facsimile of the autograph may have been published; the city, publisher, and date of the first edition; and the separate movement titles in each.[13]

Some readers will be interested in the grouping of the "thirty-two" in the eight monthly recitals alluded to above, especially as that grouping itself has a certain bearing on this introductory overview. The object was not to follow the chronological order but to find a new grouping that not only would make each recital run about the same length (75 minutes) and satisfy the special predilections of the individual performers but, as nearly as could be worked out, would include works both early and late, major and minor, familiar and less familiar, difficult and less difficult, long and short, and serious and gay.[14] The grouping that finally was decided upon follows on p. 20 (with the usual upper- and lower-case letters for major and minor keys, respectively).

[12] For a survey of the background and circumstances of these and his duo sonatas see Newman/*Classic*, especially pp. 501–43.

[13] The most convenient source for more information on each of these topics is Kinsky & Halm/*Beethoven*.

[14] Although by then the working out of the groupings had been at least tentatively completed, a kind invitation was accepted to have this problem programmed on a large up-to-date computer, with the solution to be fed back "almost instantaneously." But alas, the effort failed after prolonged attempts over a period of several months, reportedly because the computer required a larger fund of sonatas from which to choose, and could not be made to use up every and only every sonata's set of characteristics that was fed into it. To be sure, those who dread an ultimate conquest of man by machines may see in this failure at least a momentary, upset victory for man and at least one brief triumph for the arts in general!

Beethoven's Thirty-Two Piano Sonatas and Their Separate Movements

Op./no.	Key	Original (or acquired) name	Composition dates (*at latest)	Autograph Where?	Autograph Facsimile published?	First publication	Type and Order of Movement
2/1	f		*1795	lost	—	Vienna: Artaria, 1796	Allegro; Adagio; Menuetto:Allegretto; Prestissimo
2/2	A		1795	lost	—	Vienna: Artaria, 1796	Allegro vivace; Largo appassionato; Scherzo: Allegretto; Rondo:Grazioso
2/3	C		1795	lost	—	Vienna: Artaria, 1796	Allegro con brio; Adagio; Scherzo: Allegro; Allegro assai
49/1	g		1795–98	lost	—	Vienna: Bureau, 1805	Andante; Rondo: Allegro
49/2	G		1795–98	lost	—	Vienna: Bureau, 1805	Allegro ma non troppo; Tempo di Menuetto
7	Eb		1796–97?	lost	—	Vienna: Artaria, 1797	Allegro molto e con brio; Largo, con gran espressione; Allegro; Rondo:Poco allegretto e grazioso
10/1	c		1796–98	lost	—	Vienna: Eder, 1798	Allegro molto e con brio; Adagio molto; Finale:Prestissimo
10/2	F		1796–98	lost	—	Vienna: Eder, 1798	Allegro; Allegretto; Presto
10/3	D		1796–98	lost	—	Vienna: Eder, 1798	Presto; Largo e mesto; Menuetto:Allegro; Rondo:Allegro
13	c	Sonate pathétique	1798–99	lost	—	Vienna: Hoffmeister, 1799	Grave, Allegro di molto e con brio; Adagio cantabile; Rondo:Allegro
14/1	E		*1798–99	lost	—	Vienna: Mollo, 1799	Allegro; Allegretto; Rondo:Allegro comodo
14/2	G		1798–99	lost	—	Vienna: Mollo, 1799	Allegro; Andante; Scherzo:Allegro assai
22	Bb		1799–1800	lost	—	Vienna: Hoffmeister, 1802	Allegro con brio; Adagio con molta espressione; Menuetto; Rondo:Allegretto
26	Ab		*1800–01	Berlin	Bonn, 1894; scarce	Vienna: Cappi, 1802	Andante con variazioni; Scherzo:Allegro molto; Marcia funebre sulla morte d'un eroe; Allegro
27/1	Eb	Sonata quasi una fantasia	1800–01	?	—	Vienna: Cappi, 1802	Andante, Allegro; Allegro molto e vivace; Adagio con espressione; Allegro vivace
27/2	c♯	Sonata quasi una fantasia ("Moonlight")	1801	Bonn	Vienna, 1921; scarce	Vienna: Cappi, 1802	Adagio sostenuto; Allegretto; Presto agitato
28	D	("Pastorale")	1801	Bonn	None	Vienna: Bureau, 1802	Allegro; Andante; Scherzo:Allegro vivace; Rondo:Allegro ma non troppo

No.	Key	Nickname	Composed	Autograph	Facsimile	First edition	Movements
31/1	G		1801–02	lost	—	Zürich: Nägeli, 1803	Allegro vivace; Adagio grazioso; Rondo: Allegretto
31/2	d	("Tempest")	1801–02	lost	—	Zürich: Nägeli, 1803	Largo, Allegro; Adagio; Allegretto
31/3	E♭		1801–02	lost	—	Zürich: Nägeli, 1804	Allegro; Scherzo:Allegretto vivace; Menuetto:Moderato e grazioso; Presto con fuoco
53	C	("Waldstein")	1803–04	Zürich (now in Bonn)	Bonn, 1956	Vienna: Bureau, 1805	Allegro con brio; Introduzione:Adagio molto; Rondo:Allegretto moderato
54	F		1804	?	—	Vienna: Bureau, 1806	In tempo d'un menuetto; Allegretto
57	f	("Appassionata")	1804–05	Paris	Paris, 1927; scarce	Vienna: Bureau, 1807	Allegro assai; Andante con moto; Allegro ma non troppo
78	F#		1809	Zürich (now in Bonn)	Munich, 1923; scarce	London: Clementi, 1810	Adagio cantabile, Allegro ma non troppo; Allegro vivace
79	G		1809	Zürich (now in Bonn)	None	London: Clementi, 1810	Presto alla tedesca; Andante; Vivace
81a	E♭	Les Adieux, L'absence, et Le Revoir, Sonate caracteristique	1809–10	Vienna (first mvt.)	None	London: Clementi, 1811	Les Adieux:Adagio, Allegro; L'absence: Andante espressivo; Le Revoir:Vivacissimamente
90	e		1814	London	None	Vienna: Steiner, 1815	Mit Lebhaftigkeit und durchaus mit Empfindung und Ausdruck; Nicht zu geschwind und sehr singbar vorgetragen
101	A		*1816	Switzerland	None	Vienna: Steiner, 1817	Etwas lebhaft und mit der innigsten Empfindung; Lebhaft, marschmässig; Langsam und sehnsuchtsvoll; Geschwind, doch nicht zu sehr, und mit Entschlossenheit
106	B♭	("Hammerklavier")	1817–18	?	—	Vienna: Artaria, 1819	Allegro; Scherzo:Assai vivace; Adagio sostenuto: appassionato e con molto sentimento; Largo, Allegro risoluto, Fuga a tre voci, con alcune licenze
109	E		1820	Washington	?	Berlin: Schlesinger, 1821	Vivace, ma non troppo; Prestissimo; Gesangvoll mit innigster Empfindung
110	A♭		ca. 1821	Berlin	Stuttgart, 1967	Paris: Schlesinger, 1821	Moderato cantabile molto espressivo; Allegro molto; Adagio ma non troppo, Fuga: Allegro ma non troppo
111	c		1821–22	Berlin	Munich, 1922, and others	Paris: Schlesinger, 1822?	Maestoso, Allegro con brio ed appassionato; Arietta:Adagio molto semplice e cantabile

The "Thirty-Two" Grouped in Eight Recitals

Recital I: Opp. 14/2 in G, 31/2 in d, 2/1 in f, and 101 in A.
Recital II: Opp. 10/2 in F, 110 in A♭, 2/2 in A, 57 in f.
Recital III: Opp. 2/3 in C, 27/2 in c♯, 49/1 in g, 49/2 in G, 109 in E.
Recital IV: Opp. 13 in c, 7 in E♭, 111 in c.
Recital V: Opp. 10/1 in c, 10/3 in D, 54 in F, 31/1 in G.
Recital VI: Opp. 26 in A♭, 78 in F♯, 79 in G, 28 in D, 81a in E♭.
Recital VII: Opp. 14/1 in E, 22 in B♭, 90 in e, 53 in C.
Recital VIII: Opp. 27/1 in E♭, 106 in B♭, 31/3 in E♭.

Finally, to conclude the orientation, our opening definition might be elaborated upon enough to say that the field of performance practices concerns all those contemporary stylistic considerations and all those decisions that still must be made before the most faithful version available of the composer's score can be translated into the sounds of actual performance. Insofar as topics like ours are concerned, such considerations and decisions usually include the determination of a particular tempo, the realizations of symbols for ornaments, the choice and preparation of the instrument, the uses of the pedals, the marking-off of phrases and shorter ideas, and the degree of rhythmic and expressive freedom.

2

Autographs
and Editions
of the Sonatas

WHAT ARE THE SOURCES FOR INFORMATION ABOUT PERFORMANCE PRACTICES in Beethoven's piano sonatas? The present book is largely confined to information that is firsthand or at least contemporary with Beethoven. That restriction is not intended as any blanket derogation of another kind of literature on how to play Beethoven—that is, the vast literature that has streamed forth from performers, teachers, and other devotees of the master ever since he died. Although a substantial portion of that literature does sometimes seem superficial or ill-founded or both, a fair portion remains that reflects keen penetration, broad experience, and a high order of musicianship—for example, the *Introduction to the Performance of Beethoven's Piano Works* by Adolf Bernhard Marx, originally published in 1863[15]; or the annotations in Donald Francis Tovey's three-volume edition of the sonatas, originally published in 1931. But before the explorations into the performance problems can be carried further, or even defended as far as they have

[15] The original German title is *Anleitung zum Vortrag Beethovenscher Klavierwerke.*

been carried to date, it is essential to discover what bedrock evidence (if that term is not too positive) was left by the composer himself or by those associated closely with him in his profession. Our chief sources then become, roughly in order of priority: the original music itself; Beethoven's own words about it; contemporary reports of his concern with the sonata, including his own studies, playing, teaching, and music-making; and information about the pianos he used and preferred.

The primary sources are, of course, Beethoven's autographs and the editions published while he was still alive. Since all thirty-two sonatas appeared in print soon after completion (as the foregoing chart shows) and since Beethoven himself supervised at least one early publication of each (with increasing care in his later years), the question often arises, when differences occur, as to whether more weight should be attached to the reading in the autograph or to that in the early edition. And differences do occur.

For example, in the finale of Op. 109 the autograph seems to show a slur in each hand extending from the start of measure 5 through the first beat of measure 7, with a new slur starting on the next beat in the right hand—"seems," because the starting and ending points of the slurs are ambiguous, as they so often are in manuscripts (Ex. 1).

Ex. 1.   From the autograph of Op. 109, start of the finale.

But the original printed edition has the slurs ending at the barline of measure 6, and a new slur at the *start* of measure 7 (quite apart from further differences in the articulation of these measures among the leading modern editions). Much as writing about such variations may seem like hairsplitting, the altered difference in effect when the two versions of this intensely expressive music are played is considerable. Many will prefer the autograph reading.

But alas, that question of autograph versus early edition today arises in not even half of the thirty-two sonatas, largely because Beethoven took such poor care of his own autographs—showed no interest in them, in fact[16]—that only thirteen of these survive or can be found, as listed on the foregoing chart. To be sure, even though none of the early sonatas (through Op. 22) survived, perhaps we should recall how much less completely the sonata autographs of Haydn and Mozart come down to us and rejoice in what we do have of Beethoven. Slightly more than half of Beethoven's existing autographs have been made more or less available in published facsimiles, one clue to their availability being prices that start as low as two dollars (for a new facsimile of Op. 111, at that[17]), and range to as high as the traffic will bear (for scarcities already old themselves, like the facsimile of Op. 26).

What would not be given if some of the other autographs were to turn up again, as is always possible, or even just the missing first page of the extant "Moonlight" autograph! Of course, miscellaneous sketches are known for a few of the sonatas whose autographs are lost, including Op. 106. Those sketches occasionally help with some detail or other of performance practices, although one can never be sure whether exactly this detail was not revised between the sketch and the early edition that must be used for today's best editions in the absence of the autograph. A case in point is the celebrated question of A♮ or A♯, leading into the recapitulation of the first movement of Op. 106, which is argued in the footnotes of every responsible edition, often at length. The best support for A♮ lies in the harmony outlined in the sketch (Ex. 2), whereas support for A♯ lies in the

Ex. 2. From a sketch of the retransition to the recapitulation in the first movement of Op. 106 (as printed in Nottebohm/*Zweite*, 126).

---

[16] See Wegeler & Ries/*Beethoven*, 113; also, *Acta Musicologica*, XXII (1970), 43 (Lewis Lockwood).
[17] New York: Dover, 1968 (in reduced size).

two earliest editions.[18] The question becomes a performance problem
only in the sense that every performer still must decide for himself
when he plays the passage involved. Like past editors, the editors of
the two leading editions today are divided between the sharp (Ex. 3)
and the natural.[19]

Ex. 3. From a leading modern edition of the completed passage sketched
in Ex. 2 (Wallner/*Beethoven*-m, II, 234).

A-sharp or A-natural?

The first editions of Beethoven's sonatas are rare today[20] and have
not been made more available through published facsimiles. Hence it
is difficult at best to check whether the autograph or an early edition
was preferred as the source for some particular in the modern editions.
Moreover, the editors of even the best of the modern editions have
hardly attempted to indicate every decision in this regard. Beethoven
himself had found fault with the contemporary editions, trying in
vain in 1816, 1824, and 1826 to get better, complete versions of his
works published.[21] Primarily he wanted to offer more help with interpretative problems, but he had structural changes in mind, too (as
noted near the end of the present book). He did succeed in getting
Simrock to publish an "édition très correcte" of Op. 31, No. 1, in G
major, after raging over the well-known insertion of "four" (really
three) gratuitous measures by the Swiss publisher Nägeli in the first
edition, presumably to achieve a more symmetrical phrase design
(Ex. 4).

[18] The argument still goes on. For example, the natural is defended in *Neue
Zeitschrift für Musik*, CXIX (1958), 708 (H. Keller) and Ludwig Misch, *Neue
Beethoven-Studien und andere Themen*, Munich: G. Henle, 1967, 116–23; the
sharp is defended, in the most extended systematic analysis to date, by Richard
Hauser in *Beethoven-Jahrbuch*, VI (1965–68), 243–59. Tovey had concluded earlier,
on the basis of the sketch, that "though Beethoven certainly did not think of it
[A♯], he would have been delighted with it if someone had pointed out to him
that he had actually written it!" (Tovey/*Beethoven*-m, III, 139).
[19] Schenker & Ratz/*Beethoven*-m, IV, 518.
[20] Nearly every one of the "thirty-two" is represented in first editions in the
Paul Hirsch Library, acquired by the British Museum in London in 1946 (see the
listings in Vol. IV of the *Katalog der Musikbibliothek Paul Hirsch*, Cambridge:
University Press, 1947).
[21] See Schindler & MacArdle/*Beethoven*, 95–96, 400–405, 442–45.

Ex. 4. The "four" measures inserted by Nägeli in the coda of the first movement of Op. 31, No. 1 (after Wegeler & Ries/*Beethoven*, 88–90).

[present measure 299]

By suggesting numerous additional changes in tempo, dynamics, and accentuation, Czerny implied that Beethoven had not indicated all he wanted in the markings he put in his scores.[22] But these additions are little more than the usual pushes and pulls at cadences, the rises and falls in phrases, the projections of significant tones, that any musicianly player would expect to employ. For example, Czerny calls for a slight ritardando and crescendo to be introduced from the fifth measure of Op. 2, No. 1, to the hold ending the first phrase (Ex. 5).[23] And he

Ex. 5. From the opening phrase of Op. 2, No. 1 (after Wallner/*Beethoven*-m, I, 6).

calls for accents on each downstem bass note during one occurrence of the refrain in the finale of Op. 7, just before the abrupt shift from E♭ to B major (Ex. 6).[24] Schindler makes even more of the idea that

Ex. 6. From the finale of Op. 7 (after Wallner/*Beethoven*-m, I, 94).

[22] Badura-Skoda/*Czerny, passim.*
[23] Badura-Skoda/*Czerny,* 27.
[24] Badura-Skoda/*Czerny,* 33 (with ex.).

Beethoven indicated but a small portion of what he wanted in his markings, and goes on, as will be noted shortly, to urge liberties in the tempo, meter, and expressive sense that must strike most performers today as excessive to the point of eccentricity, if not downright unmusicality.

Apart from such minor revisions and changes of editorial policy as may be expected when the piano sonatas come out in the new collected edition, the best modern editions, as viewed here, are likely to remain the comparatively recent ones prepared by Heinrich Schenker and revised by Erwin Ratz, in 1946–47, for Universal Edition, and by Bertha Wallner, in 1952–53, for G. Henle Verlag. Since each of these editions aims similarly at providing the best *Urtext*, the main differences, aside from footnotes and from superior engraving in the Henle edition, lie in which sources have been preferred, with Schenker and Ratz leaning more often toward the autographs and Wallner toward the earliest editions. In faithfulness to the sources Wallner seems to have a slight edge. Both editions reveal a reluctance to accept some of Beethoven's slurs, especially the Schenker and Ratz. And we shall see presently that some of these slurs do prove hard to accept. Yet it is well to remember that, as difficult as his autographs are to read, Beethoven paid close attention to the details of his publications. Especially in later years he wrote fussy letters that itemized his corrections minutely, with regard to graphic and verbal indications as well as notes.[25]

[25] See, for example, his letters of March 8, about March 20, and April 16, 1819, including corrections of Op. 106 (translated in Anderson/*Beethoven*, II, 793–807).

3

Comments
By and About
Beethoven

CONTINUING WITH SOURCES THAT CAST LIGHT UPON BEETHOVEN PER-
formance practices, we must next take brief note of what the composer
himself had to say, as well as his closest contemporaries. Judging by
what has survived, whether in Beethoven's letters, in the remarks
credited to him by contemporaries who left memoirs, or in the so-
called Conversation Books (to the extent that the deaf composer's
unwritten responses can be inferred), he left no extended discussion of
performance practices, only nuggets here and there. These nuggets are
enough to indicate his urgent concern with performance problems,
especially tempo and expressive import. Thus, nothing is more touch-
ing in its way than the virtual legal contract, only half humorous, that
Beethoven, by then totally deaf, felt compelled to make the members
of the Schuppanzigh Quartet sign in March, 1825, guaranteeing their
best performance efforts:

Most Excellent Fellows!
   Each of you is receiving herewith his part. And each of
you undertakes to do his duty and, what is more, pledges

himself on his word of honor to acquit himself as well as possible, to distinguish himself, and to vie in excellence with the others.

Each of you who is participating in the said undertaking must sign this paper. . . .[26]

Greater fidelity to the score was undoubtedly one of the results Beethoven hoped to achieve with that document. Yet he himself is reported on at least a few occasions to have recommended departures from his own scores, one occasion being his approval of some double-notes for greater brilliance in the rondo finale of Op. 13.[27]

Remarks attributed to Beethoven on the programmatic content of his music, especially those by Schindler, have to be read more cautiously. One such was the well-known answer, "Just read Shakespeare's *Tempest*," after Schindler asked for the meaning—in the same breath, apparently—of both Op. 31, No. 2, and Op. 57.[28] However, there is no reason to question still another category of Beethoven's own words, which is the series of annotations he jotted down in an edition of selected piano etudes by Cramer.[29] The immediate purpose of these annotations was to guide Czerny in his teaching of Beethoven's unhappy nephew Karl. But Schindler concluded that they were at least a foretaste of explanations Beethoven had wanted to write for his complete edition that never materialized, or even for a piano method he had contemplated writing.[30] The annotations concern problems of accentuation and projection almost exclusively, as will be illustrated later, in our probing into articulation.

The number of Beethoven's contemporaries who wrote about him—everything from light reminiscences to serious discussions—is considerable. (Unfortunately, there is still no collection of contemporary documents for Beethoven comparable to what Otto Erich Deutsch did so well on either side of him for both Mozart and Schubert.[31]) Of these contemporaries, three stand out in all aspects of Beethoven's life, including performance practices, because they were closest to him in both his daily living and profession, and collectively, throughout much of his career. In chronological order, the first of them was Ferdinand Ries, who was especially close in Beethoven's earliest and middle years, and remained in touch later, although the relationship cooled a bit after Ries moved to London. The sources for Ries's remarks are two-

[26] As translated in Anderson/*Beethoven*, III, 1182–83.
[27] Wegeler & Ries/*Beethoven*, 106–7 (unless Ries meant his reference to double notes to apply only to the finale of Beethoven's Concerto Op. 15).
[28] Schindler & MacArdle/*Beethoven*, 406.
[29] As discussed later here and in more detail in Newman/*Cramer*.
[30] Schindler & MacArdle/*Beethoven*, 379, 414 fn.
[31] Much sifting, consolidating, and collating is needed in the various collections of L. Nohl, A. Kalischer, F. Kerst, and A. Leitzmann. Dr. Eva Badura-Skoda at the University of Wisconsin is preparing a selected collection (as of 1970).

fold: his letters to Beethoven when they can still be found, and his much cited recollections, published, soon after his death, with those of Wegeler in 1838.[32] The recollections are in the nature of witty vignettes, yet they inspire reasonable confidence in their accuracy.

Second in order was Carl Czerny, who first came to Beethoven around 1800 as a talented pupil about ten years old. Virtually all of Czerny's important writings on the performance of Beethoven's piano music are collected by Paul Badura-Skoda in a recent book published by Universal Edition.[33] These include portions of his autobiographical recollections written in 1842,[34] some other reminiscences, and, above all, the pertinent sections of his four-volume "Piano Method," Op. 500, published between 1837 and 1846. Among other things, Op. 500 contains brief but often specific discussions of each of the Beethoven sonatas. These discussions are most important for the eleven sonatas Czerny evidently learned or at least played under Beethoven's own eye—Opp. 13, 14/1, 14/2, 26, 27/2, 31/2, 31/3, 53, 81a, 101, and 106[35] —and for the earlier sonatas in general. Czerny's skimpy, superficial remarks on the late sonatas other than Op. 106 reveal his disinclination, or perhaps inability, to follow Beethoven in the composer's later years. Many of the remarks on the earlier sonatas are superficial, too, either because they merely emphasize what the player finds in the score already, or because they are too general to be tangible. Thus, of the first movement of Op. 14, No. 1, in E major, Czerny wrote,

> This movement has a cheerful noble character and should be played with life and feeling. The middle section (from m. 23 [that is, what was eventually called the second theme; Ex. 7]) should be played expressively but not dragged, since otherwise it would seem somewhat empty. [Make] the next melody (from m. 49 [50!, in the closing group; Ex. 8]) tender and harmonious. Also in this section, alternate the ideas in a descriptive-poetic manner and, indeed, create a small but rich painting.[36]

Ex. 7. From the first movement of Op. 14, No. 1 (after Wallner/*Beethoven*-m, I, 164).

---

[32] Wegeler & Ries/*Beethoven*.
[33] Badura-Skoda/*Czerny*. English translation scheduled for publication by Theodore Presser in 1971.
[34] Translated in *Czerny*.
[35] See Badura-Skoda/*Czerny*, 9, which also lists Op. 28/i; on pp. 52–54 Czerny's remarks on Op. 57 suggest Beethoven's direct influence in that work, too.
[36] Translated from Badura-Skoda/*Czerny*, 38.

Ex. 8. From the first movement of Op. 14, No. 1 (after Wallner/*Beetho-ven*-m, I, 165).

On the other hand, many of Czerny's remarks, including some noted earlier and others yet to be noted, do have meaning enough. What is more, they have a ring of authority, what with their judicious restraint and Czerny's unassailable reputation for loyalty, industry, and moral uprightness.

Anton Schindler, the third of our three contemporaries, was the first important biographer of Beethoven. The biography he left originally appeared in 1840–42, in German, English, and French editions successively, and again in 1860, in its much improved third edition. Today it is available in a new English translation (by Constance Jolly) with full and valuable annotations by the late Donald Mac-Ardle.[37] As a source for Beethoven performance practices, this book is less comprehensive in its treatment of specific works than Czerny's contributions but more penetrating in its discussions, especially of rhythmic principles, poetic content, and expressive or declamatory freedom. Because Schindler explored the whole man and explored much deeper, his must be adjudged the most important contribution by the three contemporaries. Schindler himself loudly proclaimed the need for spreading the true way to play Beethoven and his own position as the only survivor who retained that secret.[38]

But at once four serious qualifications of Schindler's contribution need to be recorded. First, he entered Beethoven's sphere only at the time of his last sonatas. Second, Schindler was not a professional musician on the level of Ries or Czerny, and certainly not their equal as a pianist, for he was primarily a lawyer and writer, next a violinist, and only lastly a pianist. Third, he committed not a few errors of fact. And fourth, he was by no means an impartial observer. Being a Boswell to Beethoven and an idolater, he was jealous of all other close associates of the master, *especially* Ries and Czerny. His jealousy shows in opinions that are frequently slanted and in his espousal of some principles that now seem eccentric. No discussion of Beethoven performance practices is likely to be complete without reference to Schindler, nor is that reference likely to be safe without some qualification or other.

[37] Schindler & MacArdle/*Beethoven*, with further details about the biography itself on pp. 19–36.
[38] Schindler & MacArdle/*Beethoven*, 396–97 and 445–46 (fn. 318).

4

Beethoven's Own Teaching and Playing

BEETHOVEN DID RELATIVELY LITTLE PRIVATE TEACHING OF PIANO—OR OF composition either, for that matter. What little he did hardly could have been anything less than superb in the inspirational sense, considering the deep impression of strength and creative genius he seems to have made on nearly all who came into close contact with him. Moreover, there is evidence to show that he took this teaching seriously, sparing no pains to make it effective, especially in its musical goals, but often in its technicalities too.[39] Ries tells of one occasion when Beethoven had him play a variation right through seventeen times because he was not satisfied with the "feel" of a particular passage.[40] Of course, when there was a pressing rehearsal or when Beethoven found himself in the heat of composing, the lesson had to go by the board.[41] Whether he could be called a master teacher in the sense of methodical pedagogy is another question. One has to remember that

[39] See the recollections in Huber/*Beethoven*, 12–13 and 29–30.
[40] Wegeler & Ries/*Beethoven*, 94.
[41] See Wegeler & Ries/*Beethoven*, 99.

in his own youth Beethoven had been too intransigent to accept fully
the composition instruction he had received from Haydn and possibly Mozart,[42] even though they were to influence his music more than
any other composers. But it is also well to remember that more than
once Beethoven declared his intention of writing his own piano
method.[43]

Probably Beethoven's best teaching in the sense of methodical
pedagogy occurred in what he prescribed for his nephew Karl by way
of Czerny. Besides his annotations in the Cramer etudes that are to be
discussed later, we get a sample in an oft-cited letter of 1817 to Czerny
about Karl's study, of which the most pertinent sentences are repeated
here:

> In regard to his playing for you, as soon as he has learned
> the right fingering and can play a piece in correct time and
> the notes, too, more or less accurately, then please check him
> only about his interpretation; and when he has reached *that
> point,* don't let him stop playing *for the sake of minor mis-
> takes,* but point them out to him when he has finished playing
> the piece. Although I have done very little teaching, yet I
> have always followed this method. It seems to produce *musi-
> cians,* which, after all, is one of the chief aims of the art, and
> it is less tiring for both master and pupil. In certain passages,
>
> such as ♫ I should like him
>
> also to use all his fingers now and then, and in such passages
>
> too as ♫ *etc.* ♫
>
> so that he may slip one finger over another. Admittedly such
> passages sound, so to speak, as if they were "played like pearls
> (i.e., with only a few fingers) or like a pearl"—but occasionally
> we like to have a different kind of jewelry.[44]

Beethoven's own playing was his professional mainstay at first, his
success being primarily for his remarkable improvising. The playing
began to taper off as the deafness grew, from 1802 on, becoming at
the same time rougher and less worked out. His last known appearance
at the piano outside of the privacy of his composing room was in 1814,
and he had generally stopped playing in public about five years
earlier.[45] The contemporary reports on Beethoven's piano playing are

[42] See Schiedermair/*Beethoven*, 182–89.
[43] See Huber/*Beethoven*, 11; Schindler & MacArdle/*Beethoven*, 379–80, 400, 420.
[44] As translated in Anderson/*Beethoven*, II, 742–43. Evidence that Beethoven's
attention to fingering was of long standing is cited (from 1787) in Huber/*Beethoven*,
11.
[45] See Schindler & MacArdle/*Beethoven*, 171, 173, 413, 416, 417.

scattered and often not specific enough to throw clear light on performance practices. Most of these reports, as well as those on his teachings, are brought together in a useful little (and little-known) book that will be mentioned here again, originally published in 1881 as a preface to the Steingräber edition of Beethoven's Piano Concertos. It is Franz Kullak's book on *Beethoven's Piano Playing*, apparently published separately only in its English translation (by Theodore Baker), in 1901.[46]

The gist of the scattered reports is that at his best Beethoven played his allegros with great dexterity but a somewhat heavy hand, evidently meaning too few pedal changes, too much vigorous accenting, and too much animal spirits in general. However, there is no question about his masterful, soulful playing of the adagios. Reports of his playing of his own sonatas are scarce and piecemeal. But this dearth is not surprising when one recalls that only two *public* performances of his solo piano sonatas are known throughout his lifetime, neither being by him or in Vienna. One performance, either of Op. 90 or of Op. 101, was in Leipzig, and the other, of Op. 26, was—let all devotees of musical Americana take note—in Boston.[47] Reports on specific aspects of Beethoven's piano technique, except as they may sometimes be guessed on the basis of internal evidence in his music itself, cannot be found.

[46] Kullak/*Beethoven*. Another helpful source is an article in Frimmel/*Beethoven*, II, 203–71. See also Schindler & MacArdle/*Beethoven*, 79 and 413.
[47] See Newman/*Classic*, 528–29; Newman/*Beethoven*, 736.

5

Beethoven's Pianos Versus His Piano Ideals[48]

FINALLY, AMONG THE SOURCES ON PERFORMANCE PRACTICES IN BEETHO-
ven's piano sonatas, we must include what information can be found
on the pianos themselves—that is, on the pianos Beethoven used and
what he preferred in his pianos. This information has a bearing on
performance problems of pedalling, of possible extensions of the range,
of styles of touch as influenced by the hammer action, and of tone
production. Five pianos in particular are identified with Beethoven.
In the order that he first used them, they are the Stein and the
Streicher, both made in Vienna; the Érard, made in Paris; the Broadwood, made in London; and the Graf, made in Vienna. At least five
other, more obscure makes are known to have been used by him too,
including, early in his life, two pianos that, like the Stein, had been
used by Mozart before him—the Späth and the Walter, made in
Regensburg and Vienna, respectively. Of the five particularly identi-

[48] The title used for this chapter is that used for a recent article, Newman/*Pianos*,
which underlies and amplifies the subject matter introduced here, and supplies
the necessary documentation (including a separate bibliography).

fied with Beethoven, three are well known today because they—that is, the very instruments he owned—have been preserved as major treasures in three different museums. The Érard is now in the Kunsthistorisches Museum in Vienna, the Broadwood in the National Museum in Budapest, and the Graf in the Beethoven-Haus in Bonn.

The Érard piano came as a surprise gift to Beethoven in 1803 in recognition of his growing fame (Ill. 1, p. 36). Its donor was the celebrated Paris maker himself, Sebastien Érard. It has a range from contra-F to c^4, and it has four pedals: from left to right, lute (by inserting leather thongs); damper (as on today's pianos); dampening (by inserting a cloth fringe); and action-shifting (as on today's grand pianos). In 1825 Beethoven gave the Érard to his brother to make room for his new Graf piano.

The Broadwood piano came as another surprise gift in Beethoven's honor, about mid-1818, seven months after being shipped by Thomas Broadwood of London (in late 1817; Ill. 2, p. 37). It remained with Beethoven until he died, eventually coming into Franz Liszt's possession. It has a range of six octaves, from contra-C to c^4, it is triple-strung in steel wire throughout, and it has two pedals, the left for action-shifting from *tre* to *due corde* and *una corda*, and the right for damper control. But the right pedal itself is subdivided so that its left half controls the dampers from contra-C to b, and the right half from c^1 to c^4. Four legs support this heavier instrument.

The Graf piano was designed especially to help overcome Beethoven's deafness, although in vain, and was given to him in 1825 on permanent loan for the last two years of his life by the Viennese manufacturer (Ill. 3, p. 39). It has a range from contra-C to f^4, a special resonator plus quadruple stringing from great-D to the top for bigger sound, and three pedals: from left to right, action-shifting, dampening, and damper.

Among these three pianos, the Broadwood in particular helps to account for a generally accepted statement to the effect that Beethoven shifted his allegiance in the course of his career from the Viennese pianos, with their light action and delicate tone, to the English pianos, with their heavier action and more powerful tone. However, further investigation now points the other way, to the effect that Beethoven retained—in fact, never gave up—his allegiance to Viennese pianos, albeit to Viennese pianos that kept pace in their own way with current trends in size, tone, and action.[49] Indeed, for different reasons all three extant pianos owned by Beethoven must be regarded as among the least representative of his preferences among all those pianos he is known to have used. With the Érard he expressed dissatisfaction from

[49] For those interested in exploring this question further, reference is made again to Newman/*Pianos* as the support for this chapter.

Ill. 1. BEETHOVEN'S ÉRARD PIANO.

Ill. 2. BEETHOVEN'S BROADWOOD PIANO.

the start, and soon found it "useless," with its heavy action built after English models. The Broadwood similarly gave trouble at once on account of its cumbersome action, and—far from introducing a wider-ranged keyboard to Beethoven, as is usually assumed—its six octaves restricted him to a range that he had already exceeded in Op. 101 and Op. 106, and that he was to exceed again in each of his remaining three sonatas. The Graf piano did have just the range necessary to encompass all of Beethoven's piano writing, since he had had a hand in its specifications. Moreover, its tone probably approximated his tonal ideals, in spite of the peculiar effect the resonator was reported to have had. But the Graf could hardly be called representative, since it came at the end of his life, well after he had stopped playing, when he could no longer hear it at all, and well after he had already completed all his main piano writing.

Even though Beethoven frequently expressed dissatisfaction with the piano as an adequate—much less, ideal—musical instrument, his correspondence and related documents make abundantly clear that he still preferred the Viennese instruments, from his early to his last years. Especially did he favor the pianos made by various members of the Stein-Streicher family, to which he was close throughout his life (Ill. 4, p. 40). This family included Johann Andreas Stein (whom Beethoven, like Mozart, had visited in Augsburg), his son Matthäus Andreas and daughter Nannette, and the latter's husband Johann Andreas Streicher. Unfortunately, there is no Stein or Streicher piano extant that can be directly identified with Beethoven, probably because he never owned one—or indeed any other piano that was not a gift. He had no reason to buy one when the Vienna manufacturers were only too eager to have him borrow and, hopefully, endorse their wares.

If it were possible to identify particular pianos as having been used by Beethoven during the composition of particular sonatas, we might have valuable new clues on performance practices in a particular work. But besides having too little information on when he borrowed what instruments, we have the further problem that Streicher custom-made his pianos to suit each purchaser's preference and thus varied them considerably in range, pedals, action, and tone. All we can do, then, is take note of what demands Beethoven's successive sonatas make in the way of range, pedals, action, and tone, as a kind of minimum profile of what he was expecting in a piano at any one time.

As to range, the first twenty sonatas, all composed before 1803 and Op. 53, do not exceed the five octaves, from contra-F to f^3, that defined the standard limit of the 18th-century harpsichord and piano.[50] The remaining twelve sonatas gradually and irregularly extend the range

[50] The $f\sharp^3$ that crept into m. 41 of Op. 14, No. 2, first movement, surely must have been an error.

Ill. 3. BEETHOVEN'S GRAF PIANO.

ILL. 4. TWO VIENNESE PIANOS

such as Beethoven used: top, (signed) "brother and sister Stein," 1797;
bottom, Nannette [Stein] Streicher, 1819. By kind permission, respectively, of the Historical Museum in Basel and the Historical Museum
in Bern.

upward as much as an octave (to f⁴ in Op. 106) —though not down-
ward until the last five sonatas, from 1816, and then only by a fourth
(to contra-C in Op. 110 and Op. 111) . In the first twenty sonatas, as
is well known, Beethoven seems to have chafed at the five-octave limi-
tation, to judge from the numerous alterations he had to make when
he reached either top or bottom before he had completed a melodic
line. Usually the alteration shows up in the return to the idea. But
in the first movement of Op. 10, No. 3, one does not need to have
heard the closing idea before to realize that Beethoven found himself
cut short (Ex. 9) . And the proof lies, of course, in the return, where
the range does permit the line to fulfill itself (Ex. 10) .

Ex. 9.   From the first movement of Op. 10, No. 3 (after Wallner/*Beetho-*
ven-m, I, 126–27) .

Ex. 10.   From the first movement of Op. 10, No. 3 (after Wallner/*Beetho-*
ven-m, I, 131) .

The performer's option today lies in restoring or not restoring what he presumes to be the intended shape of the idea, now that the needed extensions are available. Most present-day pianists elect not to make the "restoration," presumably because they are purists by nature, because stylistic anachronisms may result from only an occasional extension of the limits, and because a certain esthetic virtue derives even from that discipline of adhering to the limits. After Beethoven's death, but still in his circle, Czerny and Schindler spoke against such changes, whereas Streicher, seeing the possibility of a new market for the same music, had already advised Beethoven to make the changes in the complete edition that he contemplated. It should be added that as early as 1803, fourteen years before Op. 106 was started and well before any English or French examples, Streicher had made pianos with a six-octave range, and that only four years later, in 1807, Beethoven was utilizing that full range in the piano transcription of his Violin Concerto in D, Op. 61. And it is interesting that as the range of pianos available to Beethoven was extended he showed less and less of that chafing at limitations, until in the last sonatas he stayed comfortably within the available range.

With regard to Beethoven's use of the pedals, a marginal note near the start of the autograph of Op. 53, seldom noticed, indicates that Beethoven was already accustomed to the divided damper pedal separating bass and treble controls, fifteen years before this mechanism came to him on his Broadwood. But there is no request for this distinction in any of his pedal markings, unless he assumed it would be made as a means of avoiding the blur that otherwise results from some of those markings. There also is no request for the dampening pedal, lute pedal, or other effect achieved by inserting cloth or other material between the hammer and string. In short, regardless of what pedals or earlier knee-action devices he had on his pianos (and to which he may have resorted in his own playing), he specified only the damper pedal and the action-shifting (or *una-corda*) pedal in his piano writing.

He specified the damper pedal only a moderate number of times and only from Op. 26 on. Prior to Op. 53 his designation for raising the dampers was "senza sordini." Czerny says he used that term only while his pianos still had a knee-action control. "Ped." was his usual designation for the foot-action control, from Op. 53 on. He used the action-shifting pedal only a few times and only in the first four of the last five sonatas, from 1816. But it is just possible that he implied other and earlier uses of it when he used the word "pianissimo," which sometimes had that meaning in his day. In any case, he had already expressed clear interest in having an "una corda control" as early as 1802.[51] Requests like that in the slow movement of Op. 106—from *una corda* "poco a poco [to] due poi tre corde"—imply a graduated action-shifting that actually reduces to two shifts, and on our present pianos to but one shift, since the triple stringing is now too close to permit the hammer to shift to *una corda*. More specific aspects of Beethoven's pedalling come up in the second part of this book, in the discussion of "The Sound Itself."

With regard to the piano actions that he used, Beethoven did not yet know the double-escapement principle introduced by Érard in 1821 (i.e., seventeen years after Érard had given Beethoven one of his instruments). Nor did Beethoven know the effect of that other important innovation during the first half of the century, the one-piece cast iron frame (from 1825). Therefore, the "main distinction in piano construction that concerns the present discussion was still that between the so-called German (or Viennese) and English actions—that is, between the German system of separately hinged keys, with its shallow, light, fast, responsive touch, leading to a highly controllable, songful yet weak tone, and the English system of suspending the keys from a common rail, with its heavier, deeper, more sluggish touch, but leading to a rounder, fuller tone of wider dynamic range."[52] That Beethoven continued to prefer the lighter action in his late works is supported not only by documentary evidence but by frequent internal evidence— for example, the open-position, broken-chord triplets, soft but extremely rapid, in the Scherzo of Op. 106 (Ex. 11).

Ex. 11.   From the Scherzo of Op. 106 (after Wallner/*Beethoven*-m, II, 241).

As for Beethoven's tonal ideals, a topic that is necessarily elusive because it depends so greatly on subjective considerations, this question will also be explored further in our discussion of "The Sound Itself."

[51] Once more, reference is made to Newman/*Pianos* for all necessary documentation in this chapter.
[52] Quoted from Newman/*Pianos*, 496–97.

6

Some Obstacles
Facing
the Researcher

AFTER THIS SUMMARY OF THE MAIN SOURCES FOR PERFORMANCE PRACTICES
in Beethoven's piano sonatas, one other type of problem needs special
mention in this first part of the book. That is the particular type of
obstacles facing the researcher of this topic, obstacles over and above
those that generally hamper any study of pre-1900 performance practices, such as the lack of a reliable tradition and the lack of contemporary phonograph recordings. All five obstacles to be mentioned
have already been hinted at here.

One such obstacle arises in Beethoven's notation and handwriting.
His manuscripts are generally harder to decipher than those of any
other great master.[53] An average, not exceptional, sample is the page
Beethoven added at the end of the autograph of Op. 53 to explain how to play the difficult so-called "Beethoven trills" in the
finale (Ex. 12.) Yet how Beethoven fumed over the mistakes of which

[53] It is illuminating to verify this statement by examination of the second volume
(plates) of *Musical Autographs from Monteverdi to Hindemith,* by Emanuel
Winternitz, New York: Dover, 1955.

Ex. 12.   From the end of the autograph of Op. 53.

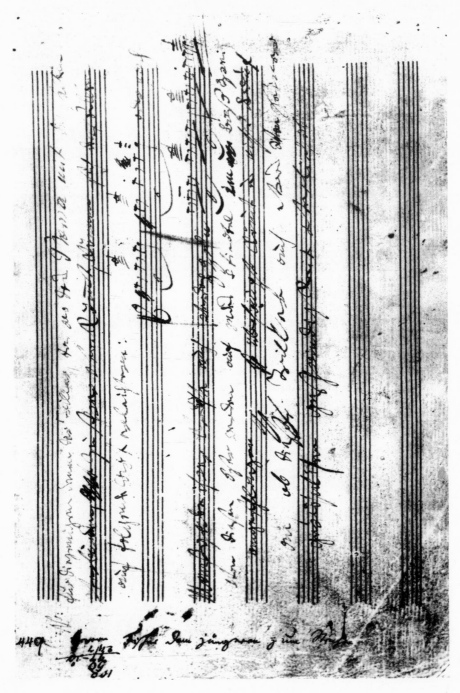

he accused his long-suffering copyists![54] Of course, most of Beethoven's works are now readily available in clear, printed *Urtext* editions, with the graphic riddles solved and made easy to read. Under these circumstances, the page just cited from Op. 53 poses no reading problem, especially when presented in translation (Ex. 13), although its appli-

Ex. 13. Part of the same page from Op. 53, printed and translated (after Kullak/*Beethoven*, 93).

or taken twice as fast, if ability permits:

cation at the piano is another matter. However, in the fussy territories explored in performance practices, the researcher likes to be able to go back to the original and see for himself.

A second obstacle is the gnawing, ever-present question of how well Beethoven actually could hear the sonority of what he was writing—that is, how much his concept of sound was disturbed by his deafness, which began by 1800, became serious by 1802 (when he wrote the well-known, suicidal Heiligenstadt Testament), and worsened except for occasional letups until it became complete during the composition of Op. 111 in 1821–22. Certainly, no one who has practiced the last five sonatas extensively can fail to be almost painfully aware of the continuing problems of balance, projection, and clear sonority. How does one digest the thick bass chords at the end of Op. 101 (Ex. 14) or

Ex. 14. From the ending of Op. 101 (after Wallner/*Beethoven*-m, II, 226).

[54] For example, see his letter of 1825 in Anderson/*Beethoven*, III, 1269–70.

bring into focus the wide spacing (mm. 118–19) of the variations in Op. 111, wide enough, as one Englishman put it, "to let a coach-and-four through" (Ex. 15)? To be sure, we do not expect the trans-

Ex. 15. From the second movement of Op. 111 (after Wallner/*Beethoven*-m, II, 325).

parent clarity of Mozart's Classic piano writing before Beethoven, or even of Chopin's remarkably euphonious writing after him. Beethoven's instrument itself was in too uncertain a state of transition, and his late masterpieces are often experimental—experimental in the sense that has inspired the occasional epithet "magnificent failures." For that matter, Beethoven's evident temperament suggests that he may not have meant the sound to be beautiful at all times (as Mozart is said to have insisted it be). In some passages, for example, the sounds seem deliberately to be made unbeautiful by the harshness of the dissonance, especially when that dissonance is thrown into bold relief by a stark, open, spare texture (Ex. 16). In that connection

Ex. 16. From the finale of Op. 106 (after Wallner/*Beethoven*-m, II, 261).

the layman marvels that Beethoven could continue composing after he became deaf. The professional marvels not so much at the mental hearing, which is basic to any real professional's training, but at how, during much of his piano writing, Beethoven was creating for new instruments whose sound and range he had never been able to know without at least *some* aural distortion.

A third obstacle lies in the poor state of the Beethoven literature, which, though immense, is still the least organized of that for any of the greatest masters. A new critical complete edition of the music, as well as the first integral publication of sketchbooks, conversation books, and documents, is now envisioned in Bonn, and there is distant talk of a grand new biography to replace the monumental study by Thayer, ably brought up to date by Elliot Forbes, yet already a century old in its original form and still without discussions of the music. Only when these projects are brought to fruition will it be possible fully to evaluate and reconcile the highly divergent, even conflicting sources that bear upon the study of Beethoven performance practices.

A fourth obstacle lies in the insufficient accounts of Beethoven's own playing, insufficient especially in their lack of specific details on either interpretation or physical techniques. But that difficulty exists also for Bach and to a considerable extent even for Mozart and Chopin. At this late date the chances of discovering more details seem slim.

And a fifth, related obstacle is the large proportion of information about all facets of Beethoven performance practices that is not specific. Admittedly, the topic itself is characterized by subjectivity of the most nonspecific sort. We have seen how Beethoven cautioned Czerny not to get bogged down in technicalities and to get into interpretative matters as soon as possible. Beethoven was of the sort who said, show them the goals and they will find out for themselves how to reach them. Quite apart, then, from the fact that writing about music was much less objective then than now, we can understand why Ries, Czerny, and Schindler preferred to concentrate on what might best be called the "poetic content" of Beethoven's music. The poetic content *is* paramount, but discussions of it are not likely to occur in terms tangible enough to relate to specific performance practices.

Even so, notwithstanding the difficulties of being specific, the time has come in this little book to go beyond the sources and begin our eight sample probings into eight specific kinds of performance-practice problems in Beethoven's piano sonatas.

PART TWO

EIGHT

SAMPLE

PROBINGS

7

Tempo
and
Tempo Changes

TEMPO AND TEMPO CHANGES MUST BE THE TOPIC OF OUR FIRST PROBING
into performance practices, if only because Schindler tells us that
Beethoven himself viewed tempo as primary: "When a work by
Beethoven had been performed his first question was always, 'How
were the tempi!' Every other consideration seemed to be of secondary
importance to him"[55]—and, one might add, dependent on the tempo.

That Beethoven tried to solve the problem with the help of Maelzel's
new metronome is well known and has been much discussed. Schindler's
own long discussion comes to the conclusion still prevalent today,
though largely disproved, that Beethoven ultimately became disgusted
with the device after he found himself suggesting two contradictory
sets of tempos, on two different occasions, for the Ninth Symphony.[56]
Although Beethoven did indicate some dissatisfaction and some wav-
ering, the pioneer Beethoven scholar Gustav Nottebohm has shown

[55] Schindler & MacArdle/*Beethoven*, 423 fn.
[56] Schindler & MacArdle/*Beethoven*, 423–26.

that Schindler went too far.[57] He also caught Schindler in two main errors—one, that there were then two different sizes of metronomes whose numbers meant two different rates of speed, and the other, that Beethoven left metronome marks only for Op. 106 and the Ninth Symphony. Actually, he left marks for all nine symphonies, as well as for the first eleven string quartets and a few smaller works.

From our standpoint it does seem unfortunate that among the sonatas he left marks only for Op. 106. Or maybe it is not so unfortunate, judging by the absurdly fast tempos he prescribed for at least the first two of the three fast movements. The slow movement and the fast fugue finale seem to be on the upper acceptable limit of their possible tempos. But unless the seconds ticked by slower in those days, Beethoven simply must have lost touch with technical demands as well as sound by 1817–18. Imagine what metronome mark he might have given to the triplet section of the Scherzo (recall Ex. 11) if he had chosen to mark it too! To realize just *how* absurdly the first two movements of Op. 106 are marked, one only needs to hear the distressingly hectic recording made in blind faith as part of the complete "thirty-two" performed by Artur Schnabel.[58] (In all fairness, one should realize that Schnabel intended to redo this example of youthful idolatry, as also his relatively inexperienced edition of the sonatas.[59] His playing of the slow movement in Op. 106 has much to be said in its favor.) By general artistic consensus, Beethoven's mark of 138 per half note in the first movement has to be reduced to about 96. A tempo of 138 per quarter note, as prescribed in Beethoven's day by Moscheles, would be more likely, although then too slow. If, on the other hand and by any chance Beethoven really did mean what he said, with 138 per half note, then his tempo belies the modern conclusion that Beethoven tempos have gradually sped up over the years. In support of that conclusion, Fritz Rothschild has offered evidence that the Third Symphony took one full hour in Beethoven's day, fifty-two minutes early in this century, and forty-six minutes on a recent recording.[60] As is so often the case, arriving at a decision in questions of performance practices means "an educated guess within the known limits." The educated guess this time would continue to be that 96 per half note is still fast enough for the first movement of Op. 106.

For all the other sonatas, Beethoven's Italian inscriptions, later sometimes in German, convey much to those who can be counted on, as Brahms is supposed to have put it, to *feel* the right tempo anyway.

[57] Nottebohm/*Beethoveniana*, 126–37.
[58] Seraphim IC–6066.
[59] Artur Schnabel, *My Life and Music*, New York: St. Martin's Press, 1964, 130–31.
[60] Rothschild/*Performance*, 9.

As he wrote more sonatas, he attempted more and more to pin down the tempo in words—words ranging all the way from, for example, the simple inscription "Adagio" for the slow movement of Op. 2, No. 1, to an inscription that may be translated as "A little less andante— that is, a little more adagio than the theme" in the fourth variation of the finale of Op. 109. We do have the authority of full metronome markings in early editions by both Moscheles and Czerny, although these are contested by Schindler.[61] And Czerny, like Beethoven himself, seems fast in many instances (apart from being clearly wrong in one instance). An average of all the marks given by all the principal editors of the sonatas since Beethoven's time might have significance, were some researcher with a statistical bent inclined to compile it.

On the question of freedom of tempo, Ries says that Beethoven stayed in time fairly strictly in his own playing,[62] and Czerny implies that steady time was generally appropriate.[63] As noted earlier, Czerny's suggestions for tempo changes are largely confined to the kind of pushes and pulls at cadences that go almost without saying. Schindler, as already indicated here, stated that Beethoven played with more freedom and argued for that freedom: "His playing was free of all constraint in respect to the beat, for the spirit of his music required that freedom."[64] Of course it must be remembered that Ries and Czerny had their best opportunities to observe Beethoven during the writing of his early and middle works, and Schindler's time came later—when Beethoven was in any case writing his freest works. The tempo adjustments Schindler advocated in the slow and fast portions of the first movement of Op. 13 were numerous,[65] but he was already writing from a later viewpoint. In 1840, in the first edition of his Beethoven biography, his detailed discussion of how to play each movement of the two sonatas in Op. 14 is largely a chronicle of tempo changes and includes the statement, ". . . in every moment, Beethoven varied the tempo according as the feelings changed."[66]

But it is important to note that in 1858 Adolf Bernhard Marx reproached Schindler regarding another aspect of the same discussion,[67] whereupon Schindler took advantage of the third edition of

[61] Schindler & MacArdle/*Beethoven*, 426; see also *Music Review*, XXV (1964), 136–41 (Alan Tyson).
[62] Wegeler & Ries/*Beethoven*, 106.
[63] Badura-Skoda/*Czerny*, 30 (among other, similar implications).
[64] Schindler & MacArdle/*Beethoven*, 412; see pp. 409–412 and 417–20.
[65] Schindler & MacArdle/*Beethoven*, 420 and 497–501.
[66] Pp. 131–40 in Vol. II of Moscheles' translation (London, 1840; quoted in Harold Schonberg's *Speaking of Pianists*, New York: Simon and Schuster, 1963, 79–84). It appears in a different translation in Rothschild/*Performance*, 112–16.
[67] In the first volume of *Ludwig van Beethovens Leben und Schaffen*, p. 128 (ed. of 1902).

his Beethoven biography to renounce and delete what he had had to say about Op. 14 in the first edition.[68] Yet Schindler continued to make suggestions about freedom of tempo in the new third edition, some of them strained enough to leave one in doubt about Schindler's own musicality. The trees begin to get in the way of the forest. His object was more telling musical rhetoric and declamation. As one illustration, he recommended, in a passage early in Op. 10, No. 1, that the quarter-note rests in the right-hand staff all "be extended to about double length, and the disconnected phrases violently flung out."[69] Kullak realized this passage with added rests, without comment and perhaps more literally than Schindler intended (Ex. 17). Schindler also pre-

Ex. 17. Schindler's extended rests in Op. 10, No. 1, as realized with inserted rests by Kullak (after Kullak/*Beethoven*, 26).

[68] Schindler & MacArdle/*Beethoven*, 406–7.
[69] Schindler & MacArdle/*Beethoven*, 418.

ferred the gentler, more songful themes to give way in tempo,[70] whereas Czerny, obviously more Classic-minded, urged a change in style, not in tempo, saying that the pauses or changes of pace would confuse the listener and sacrifice the unity of form.[71]

[70] Schindler & MacArdle/*Beethoven*, 412.
[71] Badura-Skoda/*Czerny*, 30.

8

Programmatic
Content

OUR SECOND PROBING EXPLORES THE QUESTION OF PROGRAMMATIC CON-
tent in Beethoven's sonatas, with special emphasis on any poetic or
dramatic meaning that might influence or illuminate their performance. Only two of the sonatas commit the composer to any such
meaning—that is, the *Pathétique,* Op. 13, and the *Farewell,* Op. 81a,
which are the only two that bear titles originally given by the composer. All other titles that appear on our chart in Chapter 1—and
these are by no means all the titles that have been used[72]—represent
accretions after the fact (probably without Beethoven's knowledge)
in every instance, including "Moonlight" and "Appassionata."

No sonata has literal inscriptions such as Beethoven used in his
Sixth Symphony, "Pastoral." In fact, the *Pathétique,* with no subtitles at all, goes no further at most than the idea of pathos or intensive emotional experience; hence this title might apply with equal
validity to almost any of Beethoven's most serious, emotive sonatas,

[72] See Newman/*Classic,* 509.

from Op. 2, No. 1, to Op. 111. The *Farewell* does at least set the moods with its three subtitles over its three movements—"Farewell," "Absence," and "Return." But these subtitles hardly seem to justify the more detailed, literal interpretations they have brought on by way of an explicit programme. Typical is the footnote in Hans von Bülow's devoted, yet now infamous, 19th-century edition, about a passage near the start of the finale of Op. 81a (mm. 5–8) : "Even a player with the most deeply rooted antipathy to programmes cannot help seeing that in the falling pairs of thirds for the left hand the gesture of beckoning with a handkerchief—the tone-picture of a sign—is illustrated, a sign apprising the coming one of the waiting one's presence."

Such a notion is likely to bring nothing but smiles today. Yet Czerny and Schindler concur at least to the extent that Beethoven did have programmatic associations in his sonatas, quite apart from any titles. Said Czerny, for example, about the finale of Op. 57, posthumously dubbed "Appassionata":

> If Beethoven, who was so fond of portraying scenes from nature, was perhaps thinking of ocean waves on a stormy night when from the distance a cry for help is heard, then such a picture will give the pianist a guide to the correct playing of this great tonal painting. There is no doubt that in many of his most beautiful works Beethoven was inspired by similar visions or pictures from his reading or from his own lively imagination. It is equally certain that if it were always possible to know the idea behind the composition, we would have the key to the music and its performance.[73]

But, Czerny added, "Beethoven was reluctant to speak on this subject," not wishing to influence others. And Schindler cited a letter by Beethoven, otherwise unknown, in which he protested the efforts of others to find programmatic content in his or any other composer's music.[74]

Among the few programmatic associations that Beethoven actually made known to Czerny, that of a horseman galloping, in the finale of Op. 31, No. 2, is typical.[75] Unlike Schindler,[76] Czerny seems not to have been told by Beethoven of any association between this work and Shakespeare's *Tempest*. In any case, the galloping association is not likely to be evoked in the minds of most musicians by that finale, with its three-eight meter, marked "Allegretto." Might it not be evoked much sooner, for example, by the finale of the next sonata, Op. 31,

---

[73] As translated in Schindler & MacArdle/*Beethoven*, 406, from the same text that appears in Badura-Skoda/*Czerny*, 54.
[74] Schindler & MacArdle/*Beethoven*, 399–400 and 446.
[75] Badura-Skoda/*Czerny*, 48 fn.
[76] Schindler & MacArdle/*Beethoven*, 406.

No. 3, with its driving, six-eight meter in gigue style marked "Presto con fuoco" (Ex. 18)?

Ex. 18. From the openings of the finales of Op. 31, No. 2, and Op. 31, No. 3 (after Wallner/*Beethoven*-m, II, 40 and 66).

Schindler, with his references to Beethoven and Shakespeare, and with his statement that Beethoven had intended to make known the "poetic content" of each sonata in the proposed complete edition that never materialized in his lifetime, went beyond Czerny.[77] And Schindler's enthusiastic extension of these associations in turn opened the gates to an extraordinary wealth of interpretations during the next century, including products as remote as Tolstoy's melodramatic novel *The Kreutzer Sonata*, as intensely subjective as Romain Rolland's *Beethoven*, and as farfetched as the literal, detailed associations by Arnold Schering of nineteen of the "thirty-two" with some of the great masterpieces of poetry and drama.[78] Among Schering's associations, for example, are the "Appassionata," Op. 57, with *Macbeth*, the "Hammerklavier," Op. 106, with Schiller's *Maid of Orleans*, and the neglected masterpiece Op. 54 in F major with *Much Ado About Nothing*. (Was that last one *meant* to be facetious?)

When one considers all that has been written and argued about Beethoven and programmatic interpretations, one is finally compelled to ask, how would knowing the facts and conjectures actually help the performer? Would it make the "Appassionata" any more impassioned or any more of something else (since Beethoven did not bestow that

[77] Schindler & MacArdle/*Beethoven*, 400–402, 404–8.
[78] See the full list in Newman/*Classic*, 503–5.

title) ? Perhaps it helps the kind of student who responds less to objective teaching than to the purely inspirational sort, the kind who needs someone else to light his inner fires for him. Even Wagner could not do more with the sonata or the symphony in his own composing because it lacked the imagery that inspired his opera music. But there are major hazards in the fact that reactions to particular imagery or particular music are individual, not universal. It is interesting that when Czerny came to Op. 31, No. 3, in E♭, he felt no special associations, galloping or otherwise. In fact, in reference to that work, he paraphrased Beethoven's own well-known remark that the *Pastoral Symphony* was "more the expression of feeling than tone painting," by writing, "more conversational than descriptive."[79]

[79] Badura-Skoda/*Czerny*, 49.

9

The Sound Itself

TO GET AT THE PROBLEM OF THE SOUND ITSELF MEANS STARTING WITH
some idea of Beethoven's own ideal of tone. We know that from early
in his career Beethoven wanted his pianos to be capable of "singing,"[80]
that he put much emphasis on legato playing in his teaching,[81] and
that his own playing was praised for both its songfulness and its
legato.[82] And we know that the tone of the best Viennese pianos was
characterized especially by its clarity, sweetness, thinness, and pliabil-
ity, as may be heard today in the best reproductions that are appearing
of those instruments and in recordings of them.[83] Furthermore, there
is ample evidence in the sonatas themselves that Beethoven regarded
these traits as paramount, and regarded them so throughout his creative life. The mature Adagio that already graces Op. 2, No. 1, is extra-

[80] See his letters in late 1796 to J. A. Streicher, in Anderson/*Beethoven*, I, 24–26.
[81] *Czerny*, 307.
[82] Kullak/*Beethoven*, 10, 13.
[83] An example of the fine recordings is that of Beethoven's reconstructed Graf
piano (in Op. 27, No. 2) as issued recently by the Beethoven-Haus in Bonn.

ordinary for its songfulness. But so, too, are sections in the later sonatas, like the tender "arioso" phrases in the slow movements of Op. 81a and Op. 110, or the first two pages, virtually a Romantic nocturne, in the slow movement of Op. 106, or the sensitive recollections of clavichord *Bebung* in that same slow movement and the one in Op. 110. (All these sections should help, too, to confirm Beethoven's lasting preference for the Viennese pianos, rather than any pronounced swing toward the English instruments.)

Even with this much of Beethoven's ideal of tone in mind, we are still faced, in our search for tangible performance practices, with much that is intangible, elusive, and subjective. Along with the difficulties of reconstructing a past ideal too remote to recapture in full, there is the complication of Beethoven's deafness—or rather, the unorthodox scoring that seems to result from the deafness, as mentioned earlier. About all the performer can do to meet this problem and its effect on the tone production is try to find, through adroit pedalling, legato, and projection, the most favorable balance and sonority on a particular instrument, in a given room, at a certain volume, and at such-and-such a tempo. As for performance practices that pertain to tone, the clues are likely to be found at least as much through internal evidence as through any historical documentation. Two kinds of internal evidence bear most directly on the ideal of tone. One is the degree of projection or sustaining power or both that Beethoven's melodies require. The other is the nature of Beethoven's own pedal markings.

The projection and sustaining power of a tone are its means of "singing." For a melody to "sing," each of its tones must project clearly above the accompaniment and last clearly into the next tone. The greatest problems naturally arise with the longest melody tones in the slowest movements. In all of Beethoven's slow movements, late as well as early, there are remarkably few instances where a tone in the course of a melody poses a serious problem of sustaining power, even for the weak volume associated with the Viennese pianos. An early, notable exception occurs in the "Largo appassionato" movement from Op. 2, No. 2, where one step in the melody must be sustained and heard for three full beats before rising to the peak of the line (Ex. 19). In this instance, it helps that the melody is in octaves, at a forte level, in the middle range, and supported by only a moderately heavy accompaniment. Generally, such a long, undecorated tone does not find a place in Beethoven's songful slow movements, what with their accompaniments changing in rapid harmonic rhythm (as in Op. 13/ii) and their frequently florid melodies (as in Op. 22/ii/47–57).

The problem of projection is mainly the usual one of bringing out each melody tone enough, but only enough, for it to stand out and last. Beethoven, heavy-handed by nature, as we have seen, tended to pound more and more as he became less and less able to hear him-

Ex. 19. From the slow movement of Op. 2, No. 2 (after Wallner/*Beethoven*-m, I, 31).

self.[84] But forcing the tone hardly becomes necessary for others unless it be in passages where the accompaniment is thickly scored in the bass (as in Op. 106/iii/110) or where the hands separate widely, with a high thin treble tone that must "sing" over a deep, full bass tone

Ex. 20. The opening of Op. 27, No. 2 (after Wallner/*Beethoven*-m, I, 249).

[84] Cf. Newman/*Pianos*, 490, 499.

(recall Ex. 15). On today's gargantuan, iron-framed, highly resonant pianos, such thick scoring and full resonance in the bass are likely to make balance of tone even more of a problem than on Beethoven's Viennese pianos.

With the creation of Op. 27, No. 2, the "noble elegy" and "sad calm" that Berlioz found in the first movement[85] challenged the performer to a new and subtler degree of tone projection, especially in the repeated-note figures and the highs and lows of the long drawn-out phrases (Ex. 20). The greater melodic weight in this movement, achieved at the expense of less activity in the bass, suggests proportionally greater tone projection. Still further tendencies in that direction can be seen in the remarkable nocturne-like passages in the slow movement of Op. 106 and the first variation in the finale of Op. 109, in both of which the Romantic um-pah-pah accompaniment prevails (Ex. 21).

Ex. 21. From Variation I in the finale of Op. 109 (after Wallner/*Beethoven*-m, II, 281).

Mention of Op. 27, No. 2, brings up the influence of pedalling on tone, especially as its first movement has the most debatable of several controversial instructions for pedalling that Beethoven left. At the start he wrote, "This whole piece must be played with maximum delicacy and without mutes [that is, with raised dampers]," and again, "constantly pianissimo and without mutes." Unless Beethoven was calling simply for constant pedalling as needed, which seems unlikely, he was asking to let the vibrations accumulate as long as the tones lasted, an effect that Berlioz endorsed when Liszt exploited it in this movement.[86] But by 1846 Czerny recommended a change of pedal with each change of bass, noting elsewhere that much blurring was intolerable on the newer, more resonant pianos.[87] Today, on the modern piano, only an idolater like Schnabel would continue to apply Beethoven's instruction literally,[88] ethereal and wonderful as its effect may have been originally.

[85] As quoted in Chapter 1 above.
[86] Prod'homme/*Beethoven*, 126.
[87] Badura-Skoda/*Czerny*, 43, 101–2.
[88] See *The Piano Quarterly*, No. 40 (Summer, 1962), 26 (G. Kochevitsky).

Beethoven called for similarly blurred pedalling in shorter passages of several subsequent sonatas, too. In the recitative passages of the first movement of Op. 31, No. 2 (such as mm. 143–48), Liszt eliminated the blur by marking the pedal's release at the end of the first chord— this in his own edition of Beethoven's sonatas in 1857, although that edition suggests no change of Beethoven's pedal markings in Op. 27, No. 2.[89] Other well-known instances of blurring occur in the finale of Op. 53 (as at mm. 13–23) and the second movement of Op. 101 (mm. 30–34; Ex. 22). These shorter, more tolerable blurrings by the

Ex. 22.   From the second movement of Op. 101 (after Wallner/*Beethoven*-m, II. 215) .

pedal have an impressionistic flavor about them, at least on the modern piano, that recalls a statement made by Donald Tovey, "Ambiguity can be an aesthetic fact in itself."

[89] Cf. Newman/*Liszt*.

10

Articulation,
Phrasing,
and
Accenting

ANY PROBING INTO ARTICULATION BRINGS US INTO INTO ONE OF THE MOST challenging and rewarding areas in the study of performance practices in Beethoven's sonatas. Articulation, to a musician, means his identification of musical ideas, especially bits of ideas, by the way he slurs or detaches them, accents them, or otherwise demarcates them. Except for the recent little book, *Phrasing and Articulation*, in which Hermann Keller surveys all eras,[90] and except for a few, more specialized studies, the subject has received surprisingly little systematic attention. Articulation marks were used but seldom in keyboard music before Bach's time and continued to be rare in his own keyboard music. They began to proliferate in the characteristic "niceties of the Classic style," including the music of Haydn and Mozart. And they became essential, indeed, in Beethoven's autographs, as his letters to his publishers emphasize. But in spite of their quantity and obvious importance, Beethoven's articulation marks present fascinating ambi-

[90] New York: W. W. Norton, 1965.

guities, especially in the delimitations of slurs and in the various shadings of detached notes, including the distinction between dots and wedges.

Thus, the second theme in the first movement of Op. 57 has some of those vexing slurs, so prevalent in Mozart and Beethoven, that seem to contradict the lyrical sweep across the barlines by ending right at the barlines or other weak beats (Ex. 23). Most performers are forced to conclude either that the slur did not mean a clear attack-and-release to Beethoven or that, contrary to the more usual idea of broad universality in his music, he was being precious, even coy in his syntactic devices. It is still harder to accept the slurs that start and end with the barline in the accompaniment (as happens frequently in Mozart's Alberti bass). The Schenker-Ratz edition seems to be faithful to the autograph in this instance and does adhere to the slurs in the accompaniment, yet departs twice from those in the melody during this first statement of it. First, this edition adds a short slur at the start of the second measure, and second, oddly enough, it fails to maintain Beethoven's next slur across the barline but stops *its* next slur just at the barline, perhaps to be consistent with Beethoven's own slur in the first full measure.

Unfortunately, as appears in the continuation of the autograph, Beethoven himself is not consistent even within this thematic group, starting the restatement an octave higher as though he were going to carry the slur across the barline, then apparently forgetting the slurring altogether for the rest of the melody. Moreover, still other inconsistencies show up when the autograph and first edition are compared, evidently causing Wallner in the Henle edition to attempt a reconciliation of the two sources, although what she actually comes up with is a solution based more on our present-day concepts of slurring across the barline (Ex. 24). Obviously this kind of discussion quickly gets too fussy to pursue in the necessary detail. This one sampling of slurs alone will have to suffice to illustrate countless similar problems facing the editor that have to be decided one way or another, if not by him then ultimately by the performer.

With regard to dots and wedges as further signs of articulation, Emanuel Bach's celebrated *Essay* had mentioned both signs in 1753,[91] but without distinguishing between them. (It is important to note Beethoven's high respect for this bible of 18th-century performance practices and the fact that the young Czerny's first assignment under Beethoven was to read it, although its actual application to Beethoven in the eight "probings" we are making proves to be but slight.)

[91] Page 154 in William Mitchell's translation, New York: W. W. Norton, 1949.

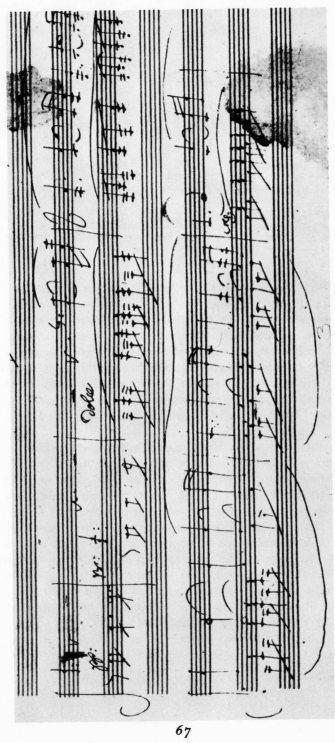

Ex. 23. From the autograph of Op. 57, first movement.

Ex. 24. From a leading modern edition of the passage in Ex. 23 (after Wallner/*Beethoven*-m, II, 132).

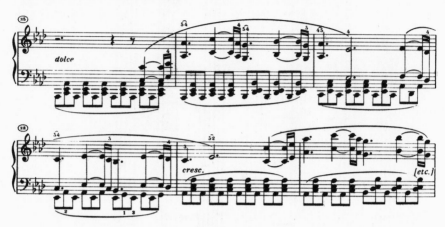

Emanuel Bach's indirect disciple Daniel Gottlob Türk did recognize that some musicians took the wedge to mean a shorter, crisper note than the staccato, in his *Klavierschule* of 1789 (page 353). Yet in Nathan Broder's careful edition of Mozart's piano sonatas, which date from the same period, the editor gave up trying to make any distinction,[92] chiefly because Mozart's autographs left the signs so hard to distinguish. Nottebohm, who contributed, as early as 1872, a chapter on Beethoven's use of dots and wedges, mustered at least tentative evidence that Beethoven did intend a distinction, starting around 1800.[93]

But whether Beethoven really meant a distinction that early is problematic, at least insofar as the autographs can tell us. Thus, in 1801, the finale of Op. 27, No. 2 has one page with clear wedges in the top brace, relatively clear dots in the third brace, and something closer to wedges in the fourth brace, partly over repetitions of the same idea (Ex. 25). In the finale of Op. 57 there are clearer instances where the same figure seems to be marked, without apparent reason, sometimes with dots and sometimes with wedges, as in the bass in Ex. 26. If one had to depend solely on such evidence one would have to join Broder in giving up any attempt to make a distinction—much as Schenker-Ratz decided in favor of nothing but wedges at both places in Op. 57, and Wallner nothing but dots!

But Nottebohm cited two further pieces of evidence proving that, at least by 1813, Beethoven did make a clear distinction. In that year

[92] New York: Theodore Presser, 1960, p. xiii.
[93] Nottebohm/*Beethoveniana*, I, 107–25.

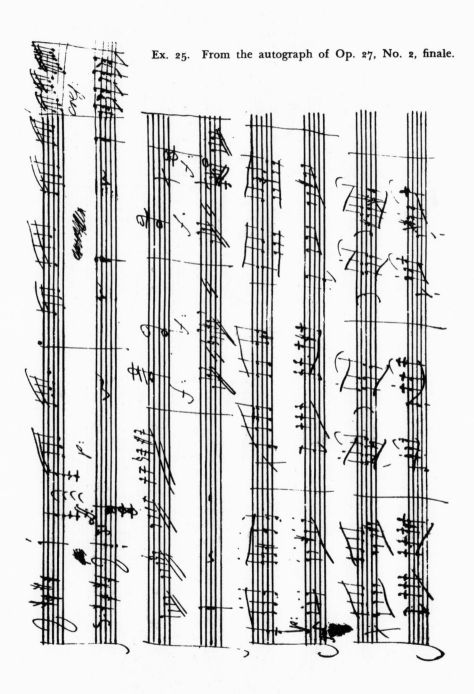

Ex. 25. From the autograph of Op. 27, No. 2, finale.

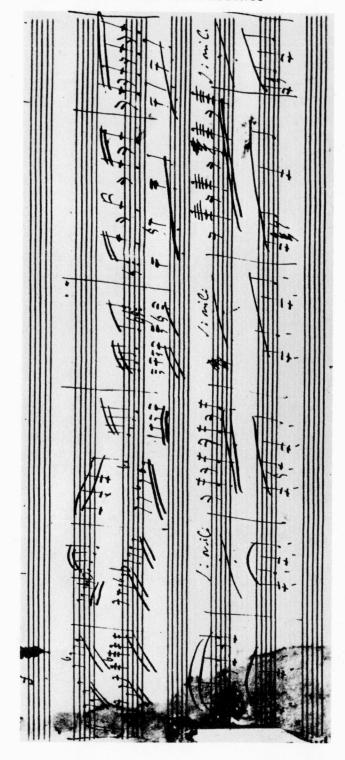

Ex. 26. From the autograph of Op. 57, finale.

Beethoven corrected a copyist's version of the second movement of his Seventh Symphony by changing the dots to wedges over the un-slurred eighth notes in the familiar theme while retaining the dots under the slurs: ♪ ♪♪ | ♪ ♪ (etc.). And in August of 1825 he wrote the copyist of his Quartet in A minor, the violinist Karl Holz, em-phasizing the distinction: "Where there is a dot above a note, a dash [wedge] must not be put instead and vice-versa— (♪♪♪ and ♩♩♩ are not identical)."[94] But, alas, he failed to add how or where the distinc-tion applies.

The conclusion reached here, based on the only internal evidence that turns up fairly often in the autographs, is that in his piano sonatas Beethoven made but one distinction with any consistency, the same one he called attention to in the Seventh Symphony. He used dots under slurs to indicate semi-detached or *portato* notes, and wedges with unslurred notes for crisper—though not necessarily the crispest possible—detachment (much as those notes with wedges in the theme from the Seventh Symphony surely are not meant to be of the crispest sort). Such a distinction between dots and wedges happens to have been made at least loosely in Leopold Mozart's *Violinschule* in 1756.[95] It is evident in Beethoven, for example, on another page in the autograph of Op. 27, No. 2 (Ex. 27).

The accenting and subgrouping of tones is a problem of performance practice that pertains quite as much to articulation as to rhythm. There is, in the early descriptions of Beethoven's own playing, at least presumptive evidence for his abundant, strong use of accents both in support of and in conflict with the meter. Thus, one can guess at such use from the opinions expressed by contemporaries who praised Beethoven's playing for its "enhanced vigor" (as against Mozart's playing), "its fiery expression," its "force and energy" (by comparison with Cramer's playing), and for being "but little cultivated, not seldom violent, like himself, but always full of spirit" (according to Clementi).[96] Czerny indicates that Beethoven often gave character and unity to a piece by accenting the recurrences of some apparently insig-nificant motive—for example, the cadential octave leaps in the bass of the refrain in the finale of Op. 26 (Ex. 28).[97] Indirect confirmation of this particular accenting comes in Beethoven's own sudden offbeat

---

[94] Anderson/*Beethoven*, III, 1241-42. The whole letter is pertinent. A facsimile of the autograph of this letter is given in Rothschild/*Performance* opposite page 100, revealing that even in this explanation the two signs are hard to distinguish!
[95] Page 213 (but see page 45) in Editha Knocker's translation, London: Oxford University Press, 1948.
[96] Kullak/*Beethoven*, 5-7.
[97] Badura-Skoda/*Czerny*, 42.

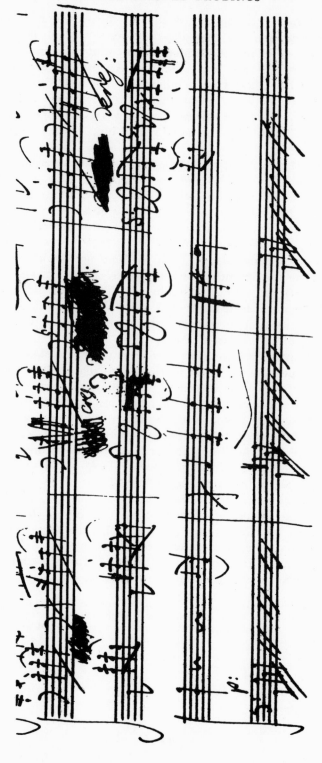

Ex. 27. From the autograph of Op. 27, No. 2, finale.

Ex. 28. From the finale of Op. 26 (after Wallner/*Beethoven*-m, I, 229).

forte on the bass octave leaps in the middle section and in the coda of this movement. Schindler says that when Beethoven taught Czerny and others, it

> was above all the rhythmic accent that he stressed most heavily and that he wanted others to stress. On the other hand, he treated the melodic accent (or grammatic, as it was generally called) mostly according to the internal requirements. He would emphasize all suspensions more than other pianists, especially that of the diminished second in *cantabile* sections.[98]

This last statement brings us to those supposed revelations of Schindler regarding what he called "the spirit inherent in the greater part of Beethoven's piano music," an apparent secret that Schindler wanted to pass on "to a later, perhaps spiritually more stable, age" lest it die with "himself as the last living member of Beethoven's circle of friends."[99] His most tangible "explanations" concern the rhetorical pauses illustrated earlier, in Op. 10/1/i (Ex. 17), and are hardly acceptable today at full face value. But he also made less tangible allusions to an interest on Beethoven's part in the stressed and unstressed accents of prosody as derived by Clementi from vocal art and

[98] Schindler & MacArdle/*Beethoven*, 416.
[99] Schindler & MacArdle/*Beethoven*, 396–97; recall Chapter 1 above.

as applied to instrumental music.[100] These allusions are made only a little clearer in Schindler's separate commentary on the annotations that Beethoven had jotted down for nephew Karl's benefit in twenty of the Cramer etudes in an early Haslinger edition.[101] There Schindler refers loosely to the Classic poetic measures: iambic, trochaic, dactylic, and spondaic. Whether he himself really got the point of Beethoven's annotations is open to question. But those annotations, which require a full discussion in themselves,[102] are almost clearer without Schindler's help, and their language is more directly related to the musician. Only a sample can be given here.

Essentially, Beethoven asks the performer to accent or carry over certain tones in order to bring out special rhythmic groupings that

Ex. 29. From Johann Baptist Cramer's Etude No. 13 in A major (after an edition by Bülow [G. Schirmer, 1875], with some accents inserted by the present author).

---

[100] Schindler & MacArdle/*Beethoven*, 414 and fn.
[101] See Schindler & MacArdle/*Beethoven*, 379, 394 (fn. 313, with mention of Shedlock's scarce publication of these notes in 1893 and Huber's recent German publication of them), and 397.
[102] They are discussed, especially as they might be applied to Beethoven's own music, in Newman/*Cramer*.

will outline and give direction to Cramer's etudes. Thus, for the Etude in A major that is No. 13 in Cramer's first collection of etudes (Ex. 29), Beethoven writes,

> The study of longs and shorts in passages is the aim here. The rhythmical accent occurs on almost all beats of the measure— for instance, from the 2d to 5th measures inclusive—[and] from the 7th to 11th measures inclusive. [One finds both] longs and shorts, the first of which I mark V, placing it under the note to be accented. Observing these longs and shorts helps the melodic movement to stand out in the passages; failing to observe them deprives every passage of its meaning.

In these annotations Beethoven does refer several times to the trochaic groupings of long and short, and once to the iambic short and long, but not to dactylic or spondaic groupings. Although no such annotations seem to have been left by Beethoven with regard to his own piano music, it is tempting—and seems justifiable enough—to apply them to similarly constructed passages in his sonatas—for example, to the bridge leading to the subordinate theme in the first movement of Op. 53 (Ex. 30). Up to the printed sforzandos, which help to

Ex. 30. From the first movement of Op. 53 (after Wallner/*Beethoven*-m, II, 89, with accents added by the present author).

confirm the principle, the accents in Ex. 30 are the present author's application of Beethoven's annotations in Cramer's etudes. But there is nothing as mysterious as Schindler would pretend about the principle. In this instance it reduces basically to an accent at every main change of direction.

11

Ornamentation

ORNAMENTATION IS THE TOPIC OF OUR FIFTH PROBING INTO PERFORM-
ance practices in Beethoven's piano sonatas. Whereas the variety of
ornamentation in Beethoven's piano writing is considerably less than
in J. S. Bach's keyboard writing, the uncertainty of its solutions is
often considerably greater. Beethoven's trills have raised the most
questions. That little book cited earlier, *Beethoven's Piano Playing*
by Franz Kullak, proceeds like a detective story in its efforts to find
the answers, especially to the question of what note to start the trill
on. But with all the interesting evidence it musters, it still often pro-
vides, by way of an answer, only an opportunity to make that "educated guess within the known limits."

Kullak attached considerable weight, for example, to the new preference for starting trills on the main note that is expressed in *The
Art of Playing Pianoforte* by J. N. Hummel.[103] This method was not

[103] Kullak/*Beethoven*, 66–87 *passim*. Hummel's book first appeared in London in
1827, in English.

published in German (Vienna, 1828) until the year after Beethoven's death, but Beethoven could well have known that gifted pianist's preferences in the matter of trills during the time the sonatas were being written, for the two men were then intimate friends.[104] How much Beethoven might have been influenced by the preferences of his friend is another question. The few clear evidences that Beethoven himself supplies are conflicting. One instance of what is presumed to be his own fingering calls for a start on the *main* note, in two trills right at the opening of Bagatelle in C major, Op. 119, No. 7 (Ex. 31).

Ex. 31. From the start of Bagatelle in C major, Op. 119, No. 7 (after Kullak/*Beethoven*, 98).

But two other instances—from the sonatas, and late ones at that— call for starts on the *upper* note, in the more traditional manner. First is Beethoven's own explanation, illustrated earlier (Ex. 13), of how the right hand can play both the trill and the theme at once in the finale of Op. 53. Second is his own fingering for a double-trill in the right hand of the second movement (m. 112) of Op. 111, as seen in the autograph (Ex. 32); the 5-4 for the upper trill, which means a start on the upper note, is clear enough; but the 1-2 below the lower trill, which means a start on the lower note, is now almost too faint to read).

Ex. 32. From the autograph of Op. 111, second movement.

[104] See Elliot Forbes, [A. W.] *Thayer's Life of Beethoven*, 2 vols., Princeton: Princeton University Press, 1964, I, 230 and II, 641.

No more conclusive are Beethoven's occasional uses of appoggiaturas to indicate the starting notes of trills. Those appoggiaturas are always the short type, they are mostly chromatic, and they always occur on the upper or lower, but never the main, note (recall Ex. 24, last brace). Among Beethoven's other means of indicating the same starts, their uses are too isolated and inconsistent to be taken as proof either that upper-note starts were the rule, with appoggiaturas used only to indicate chromatic inflections and exceptional lower-tone to indicate both upper- and lower-note starts as the exceptions. Nor starts; or that main-note starts were the rule, with appoggiaturas used can the evidence from Czerny's editing be used to prove either rule, even granting Czerny's firsthand information, for, as has been shown,[105] this evidence too is conflicting.

Lacking any better information from the composer himself, one is forced back to the conclusion that each question concerning trills must be decided on its own merits, with harmony, melody, technical fluency, rhythm, and voice leading being the main determinants. Only the general statement may be offered that harmonic and rhythmic considerations tend to favor the upper-note starts in Beethoven's early and middle sonatas, but that melodic considerations tend increasingly to favor main-note starts in the later ones. Thus, the need for harmonic dissonance and for a rhythm of six notes seems to favor upper-note

Ex. 33. From the Rondo of Op. 7 (after Wallner/*Beethoven*-m, I, 89).

starts in the trills during the first episode of the Rondo finale in Op. 7 (Ex. 33), whereas the need to emphasize the half-step rise in the fugue subject of the finale in Op. 106 favors main-note starts (Ex. 34).

There are other aspects of Beethoven's trills that call for some mention, too. For example, there is the question of how to do the so-called "Beethoven trill"—that is, the type Beethoven himself felt obliged to explain in the finale of Op. 53 (recall Exx. 12 and 13), in which the trill accompanies a melody played by the same hand.

---

[105] Kullak/*Beethoven*, 83–93; Badura-Skoda/*Czerny*, 7, 20.

Ex. 34. From the finale of Op. 106 (after Wallner/*Beethoven*-m, II, 257).

However, few pianists will accept Beethoven's clumsy solution today, even though the composer gave the option of playing sextuplets of quarter or eighth notes. One cannot help wondering how often Beethoven actually played the work himself when he composed it in 1803–04. Today the preference is almost invariably for the solution Czerny soon suggested, in which one trill note is left out each time a melody note sounds (Ex. 35).

Ex. 35. Czerny's solution to a "Beethoven trill" in the finale of Op. 53 (as illustrated in Kullak/*Beethoven*, 94).

Within the province of the trill, too, is the familiar *Pralltriller* in Beethoven's sonatas, perhaps best known in the first movement of Op. 13 (Ex. 36). Because of the fast tempo, performers are all but

Ex. 36. From the first movement of Op. 13 (after Wallner/*Beethoven*-m, I, 148).

compelled to begin this ornament on the beat and on its main note—that is, to play it in three notes, main-upper-main, moving from its accented or strongest to its weakest note. (The fast tempo similarly limits the possibilities in the first movement of Op. 7, as in mm. 209–11.) But the somewhat easier tempo in the finale of Op. 31,

No. 2, permits what, by analogy, would seem to be the wrong, less musical interpretation—that is, before the beat, moving from weak to strong, with the last note coming on the beat (Ex. 37). (Czerny

Ex. 37. From the finale of Op. 31, No. 2 (after Wallner/*Beethoven*-m, II, 40).

confused the question with the suggestion to start on the beat but to accent the third note, which solution proves almost impossible to apply.) [106]

Finally under the topic of ornamentation, the question of short and long appoggiaturas and of how long is "long," so vexing in Mozart, proves to be somewhat less vexing and less frequent in Beethoven, but it does arise. The start of Mozart's Sonata in A minor always raises doubts (Ex. 38). But thanks to what seems to be firsthand evidence

Ex. 38. From the autograph of Mozart's Sonata in A minor, K. 300d, first movement.

from Czerny[107] and to evidence in the music itself that is more obvious than Mozart afforded, we are left in little doubt as to the realization of an equally well-known appoggiatura in Beethoven, the one in the second theme of the first movement of Op. 10, No. 3 (Ex. 39). Its realization on the beat as the first of four even eighth notes grows out of the very opening of the movement and also relates to the prevailing passagework, such as the ascending scale that precedes

[106] See Kullak/*Beethoven*, 77–78.
[107] Badura-Skoda/*Czerny*, 36.

Ex. 39. From the first movement of Op. 10, No. 3 (after Wallner/*Beethoven*-m, I, 125) .

its use. Implied in its use—in fact, the apparent reason for its use—is the desire for a certain slight emphasis or dwelling on the appoggiatura note itself.

12

Dynamics
and
Expression

THERE IS PROGRESSIVELY LESS OF A TANGIBLE NATURE TO OFFER IN THE remaining three probings of this introductory book, because the problems they explore, although still very real to the performer, depend more and more on subjective considerations that must be left to the individual's own temperament and experience. Regarding dynamics and expression in Beethoven's sonatas, a first tangible observation to be made is that Beethoven marked his music more richly and consistently than any previous master—Bach, Haydn, and Mozart included—and that he marked it even more richly, with even more refinements, as the years went by. As examples of increasingly detailed instructions to the performer, Rothschild has shown that two terms, *crescendo* and *più crescendo*, alone sufficed for verbal indications of swells in Beethoven's instrumental music up to 1812, whereas at least four such terms—*crescendo, poco crescendo, crescendo poco a poco,* and *sempre più crescendo*—became necessary after 1812.[108] Similarly,

[108] Rothschild/*Performance*, 34–36.

up to 1812 five terms sufficed for gentle, expressive, songful playing—
dolce, dolce e molto legato, sempre dolce e piano, espressivo, and
molto cantabile—whereas after 1812 at least ten such terms became
necessary—*dolce, teneramente, sempre dolce cantabile, cantabile ed
espressivo, un poco espressivo, molto espressivo, espressivo e semplice,
molto espressivo e semplice, con intimissimo sentimento,* and *dolente.*

Yet even with this unprecedented wealth of editorial help, one may
assume, with corroboration from both Czerny and Schindler, that still
much more is implied and was intended in the music.[109] In other
words, much more independent responsibility is left to the performer
than the score would suggest on first inspection. But adding to the
dynamic markings and expressive directions is more than a straight-
forward editorial problem; it is a major creative challenge, and one
fraught with the dangers of inexperience and poor judgment. It
means reading between and behind the lines into the composer's
artistic intentions. In the past, the trusting performer's practice generally has been to buy this or that authority's edited version of Beethoven's text. One could then only hope that the "authority" had
not committed the cardinal editorial sin of failing to distinguish his
own editorial additions from what was in the composer's original
text—if indeed the original text had not already been corrupted.
Today, most teachers and pianists (the present author included) prefer to start with the most authentic available text and become their
own editorial authorities. If the performer, including the student,
is ready to cope with the other performance problems in Beethoven's
sonatas he should—in fact, must—be ready to meet the challenges of
dynamics and expression, too. Perhaps at least some basis for meeting
the challenge can be found in the next two observations, which suggest the need for deliberate planning rather than dependence solely on
intuitive strokes.

A second tangible observation in this chapter is that Beethoven's
dynamic and expressive indications help the interpretation not only
at the obvious local levels of phrase contrast and direction, but at the
broader structural levels as well. Thus, one notes how the dynamic
and expressive indications clarify the period directions and outlines
in the opening "Grave" of Op. 13 (Ex. 40) and how they mark off
the structural landmarks of a bridge and a closing theme in the first
movement of Op. 2, No. 3 (Ex. 41). By returning to the same dynamic
level and the same expressive directions when that phrase, or period,
or whole section is repeated, and by comparing and spacing the smaller

---

[109] Badura-Skoda/*Czerny*, 27, 28, 31, *et passim*; Schindler & MacArdle/*Beethoven*,
397–403 *passim*, 499.

Ex. 40. From the opening of Op. 13 (after Wallner/*Beethoven*, I, 146).

attacca subito il Allegro:

and bigger climaxes, Beethoven brings out the architecture of his form, a task that many regard as the prime mission of the interpreter as well.

But here a word of caution must be injected. Sometimes the indications are not parallel in corresponding phrases or larger structural sections. To take an extreme example, when the opening theme in Op. 57 returns after sixteen measures as though it is to be an identical, parallel restatement, it has barely started before it changes, with sud-

Ex. 41. From the first movement of Op. 2, No. 3 (after Wallner/*Beethoven*-m, I, 46).

den, electrifying effect, from pianissimo to fortissimo, at the same time as the texture thickens and the range expands (Ex. 42). There are

Ex. 42. From the opening of Op. 57 (after Wallner/*Beethoven*-m, II, 131).

also much less extreme examples (compare, for example, the main theme of Op. 2/2/i with its return in mm. 226–33). In such examples, we are left with the question as to whether the differences result from the composer's inconsistencies and haste, more plausible in the earlier works, or from a subtle perspective of the structural whole that most performers would need to study and acquire. If the novice working on a Beethoven sonata hesitates to face such questions (in spite of the earlier remarks here) he can find some sage musicianly advice on many of them in Donald Tovey's three-volume edition of the "thirty-two."[110]

One other observation may be made, which concerns the most frequent character of Beethoven's dynamic and expressive indications. That character is the expected one of great energy and intensive drive, much the same as was surmised earlier to be the most consistent feature of his own playing. Sforzandos, *subito* contrasts of *forte* and *piano* or more extreme markings, and expressions like "Allegro con brio ed appassionato" (Op. 111/i) —all these abound. There are also, of course, many sections that call for the gentle, expressive songfulness mentioned earlier. But at the risk of laboring the obvious in the minds of most performers, it might be well to stress that Beethoven leaves no room for the utterly placid pianist in his indications, much less in the music itself.

[110] Tovey/*Beethoven*-m.

13

Keyboard Techniques

KEYBOARD TECHNIQUES PROVIDE AN INTRIGUING FIELD FOR A PROBING, even if only a brief one, into performance practices. The reason for the brevity is our almost total lack of any knowledge of keyboard touches prior to the middle of the 19th century. Much as we have no description of Bach's playing that sheds any light on specific touches (discounting Forkel's remarks more than half a century later), nor much more on Mozart's playing, so we have virtually nothing on Beethoven's—how he held his hand, what type of finger stroke he used, whether he preferred hand or forearm action for staccato octaves, and so on. Yet we do know that Beethoven at his best was regarded by his contemporaries as a real virtuoso, and that his music itself proves him to have been a much more resourceful pianist than, for example, his great younger contemporary, Schubert. Furthermore, that oft-cited letter to Czerny on Karl's instruction, quoted earlier (p. 32), reveals a conscious concern with touches on Beethoven's part even if it does not clarify the touches themselves.

A better and fuller idea of Beethoven's approaches to the keyboard would provide valuable clues to the interpretation of particular passages, especially since he is a composer who interrelates his musical ideas and keyboard techniques so intimately. As but one example, how did Beethoven manage the rapid shifts from each one-measure slur to the next at the start of the second movement, "Allegro molto e vivace," of Op. 27, No. 1 (Ex. 43)? Did he shift the entire arm from

Ex. 43. From the second movement of Op. 27, No. 1 (after Wallner/*Beethoven*-m, I, 237).

the shoulder, locked in one piece, with each triad covered as one handful? Or did he treat the passage more like a continuous arpeggio in each hand, passing the thumbs under or over at every barline skip? The first method encourages decided separations at each barline. The second method tends to smooth out the breaks, with a very different effect, less breathless and more fluent. This latter method is supported by the possibility that to Beethoven the slurs from barline to barline meant only that legato prevailed.[111] Unfortunately, Beethoven's own fingerings are too few and too random to be of appreciable help in such problems.

Of course, in any discussion of keyboard technique we have to remember Beethoven's increasing detachment from the problems of actual performance as composing drew him away from a performer's career and as his deafness worsened. One almost gets the sense of a growing disregard on his part for such practicalities. There are several versions of the disdainful retort he is supposed to have made when the difficulties in one of his pieces were protested. But one of those versions seems particularly appropriate here—the one inspired by complaints about the third movement of his Fifth Symphony, to which he is supposed to have replied, "Do you think I think of wretched human beings when I write my string bass parts?" Whatever the reason, from the time the deafness became alarming—that is, during the composition of the three sonatas, Op. 31—there is an increasing number of what might be called blind spots or technical impracticali-

[111] Recall the start of Mozart's Sonata in B♭ major, K. 576, with its similar problem.

ties in the sonatas. Pianists struggle with these impracticalities today mainly because they take today's purist attitude and dare not contrive the more practical alternatives that Beethoven might have been only too happy to welcome in his own day had he but realized their need.

Three such impracticalities may be illustrated here. One is the very rapid leap of more than two octaves by the left hand, from across the right hand back to the bass, on the last page of Op. 31, No. 3 (Ex. 44). (The simplified scoring, whereby the right hand takes the

Ex. 44. From the ending of Op. 31, No. 3 (after Wallner/*Beethoven*-m, II, 27).

g^2 in a double-note, does away with the leap but loses the athletic and visual fun of the swish.) A second instance is the celebrated pair of scales in glissando octaves for each hand in the finale of Op. 53 (Ex. 45). Granted that glissando octaves were easier to manage on the

Ex. 45. From the finale of Op. 53 (after Wallner/*Beethoven*-m, II, 118).

slighter keyboards and with the lighter actions of the early Viennese pianos, they still are hard to control at that speed, simply because a glissando ordinarily needs to go still faster to be smooth. (The alternatives are all only fair makeshifts at best, whether staccato octaves with the damper pedal held down, fingered legato octaves for those who can play them that fast, or simple scales with the hands combining, as far as possible, on the octaves.) And a third instance that seems impractical is the cumbersome accompaniment when the main theme makes its first return in the finale of Op. 57 (Ex. 46). The figure can scarcely be made fluent enough as it stands to coordinate it

Ex. 46. From the finale of Op. 57 (after Wallner/*Beethoven*-m, II, 151).

gracefully with the right hand. Shifting it one sixteenth note either way, so that the accent falls on its inner rather than its outer notes, is only a little more convenient for the left hand. The usual out for most pianists is a loose tremolo, which possibly is all Beethoven really expected, anyway!

14

Changes
in the
Form

OUR LAST BRIEF PROBING, WHICH EXAMINES FORM IN THE SENSE OF OVER-
all design, concerns performance practices only to the extent that the
performer actually has any options with regard to the design. Those
options primarily come down to two, the possibility of reordering, or
reducing the number of, movements in the sonata cycle, and the
choice of repeating or not repeating where indications for repetition
are given.

The option of reordering or reducing the cycle, shocking as it may
seem to today's purists, does have a certain modicum of hard evidence
to support it. On several occasions, Beethoven displayed what now
seems like remarkable casualness regarding the preservation of his
cycles in their original form. For instance, there was his well-known
letter in 1819 to Ries in which, in order to insure publication of
Op. 106 in London—the mystical, magnificent Op. 106!—he wrote
that Ries could

omit the Largo and begin straight away with the Fugue . . . , which is the last movement; or you could use the first movement and then the Adagio, and then for the third movement the Scherzo—and omit entirely no. 4 with the Largo and the Allegro risoluto. Or you could just take the first movement and the Scherzo and let them form the whole sonata. I leave it to you to do as you think best. . . .[112]

There was also Beethoven's willingness to accept the suggestion that he discard the original, middle movement of Op. 53 (much as he was to be willing later to change the original fugal finale of the String Quartet in B♭, Op. 130, to a lighter movement). And there was his own tentative decision to eliminate at least a few of the scherzos from the four-movement sonatas in that proposed complete edition that never materialized.[113]

In response to these options in the cycle itself, one can only ask some questions, without hoping for final answers. Thus, since Beethoven himself seemed to have the intention—as his last word, so to speak—is the performer now justified in reducing the four-movement cycles to three-movement cycles without the scherzos? Even fortified by Beethoven's tentative intentions, would any present-day performer dare brave today's purist critics or tamper with the powerful force of tradition in this way? More important, could any devoted performer actually bring himself to sacrifice any of those uniformly fine scherzos? And what about playing only one movement from the cycle on occasion, a practice that seems to have been followed, until well into the present century, even with Classic and Romantic symphonies?

As for observing the repeat signs, there is perhaps a little better evidence that Beethoven did mean what he said.[114] Others before him had shown that the repeat signs were not introduced haphazardly, including Emanuel Bach in 1760 and Grétry in 1797. Beethoven's own editing shows that he knew very well what he was about when he did or did not insert such signs, including their elimination in certain sonata forms (among them his five most intimate examples: Opp. 27/2, 90, 101, 109, and 110), their deliberate proscription in certain internal movements (as in Op. 28/iii), and his reported concern with the question before adding a repeat sign in the first movement of his Third Symphony.

The practice of placing repeat signs around the second "half" of

[112] As translated in Anderson/*Beethoven*, II, 804–5.
[113] See Schindler & MacArdle/*Beethoven*, 402–3.
[114] For brief discussions of the question and support for the statements made here, as well as additional bibliography, see Newman/*Classic*, 114–45, 424–26, 654; Newman/*Beethoven*, 150–51.

the sonata form died out by Beethoven's time, whereas it survived in the first "half" until Brahms's time. But in today's streamlined concerts the repeat of the first "half" has often gone by the board as well, although the repeat signs in the inner movements are generally observed, and sometimes those in final movements. Occasionally the signs seem ill-advised, notably those surrounding the long section before the "Presto" in the finale of Op. 57, which few pianists have the endurance to manage even if they want to. In considering this question of repeats, perhaps least attention has been given to what should matter most: the effect on the structural balance of the movement. Thus, the usual tripartite sonata form with repeat signs at the end of its exposition offers the very differently weighted choices of A-B-A-coda and A-A-B-A-coda.

15

Some Conclusions on Changing Concepts in Beethoven Performance Practices

TO ALL WHO HAVE COME THIS FAR IN THIS LITTLE BOOK, PERFORMANCE practices in Beethoven's piano sonatas should now appear, more clearly than ever, as a set of problems whose solutions are neither finite nor final. One can usually expect by way of a solution no more than was suggested earlier, "an educated choice within the known limits."

But it is important to add that the education and the limits determining that choice can vary enough to make a substantial difference. In particular, the range of the limits can vary with the times. Looking back, we can see that this range has now come full circle, from the purist view expressed by Beethoven when he admonished Czerny for his liberties (see p. 15), to the extreme latitude represented by the Bülow edition a half-century later, and back over the next century to the narrow limits of the purist view and the antiseptic Urtext preferred today.

Recalling the still familiar Bülow edition helps to put our present views in better perspective. Hans von Bülow, the best-known editor and interpreter of Beethoven in the 19th century, in reality represented (and fully acknowledged himself to be) the fulfillment of Franz Liszt as the most influential interpreter of Beethoven in the 19th century.[115] The best representation of Liszt's interpretative ideas about the sonatas is found, as Liszt himself said more than once, in the Bülow edition, and certainly not in Liszt's own edition (1857), which, except for markings in the last three sonatas, is scarcely more than a reprint of the earliest editions. For all its freedoms and all its ill repute today, the Bülow edition was a labor of love, executed with the greatest care and, at least for a few years, almost universally endorsed. And, for all that ill repute, it is still the only edition known to many students today.

Perhaps the pendulum now has swung back too far in the direction of purism. In spite of Beethoven's objections to Czerny's liberties, he was actually more of a far-seeing early Romantic than Czerny, and in more significant ways. He experimented with new sounds, new harmonies, and new structures, and even with hidden programmatic meanings.

To be sure, such remarks take us into the realm of the speculative, where too many of the problems of performance practices already lie, of necessity. We are thus brought back to our starting point, the real need for further, extensive and intensive studies into Beethoven performance practices, so that our knowledge can at least be brought up to the level represented by the parallel studies that do exist for Bach. The present little book will remain, then, what it was meant to be at the outset, an introduction.

[115] For a discussion of Liszt's interpreting of Beethoven's piano sonatas and Bülow's role, see Newman/*Liszt*.

CHIEF REFERENCES

(A hyphenated suffix, -m, at the end of a short title means a music score.)

Anderson/*Beethoven*

Emily Anderson (editor and translator), *The Letters of Beethoven*, 3 vols. London: Macmillan, 1961.

Badura-Skoda/*Czerny*

Paul Badura-Skoda (ed.), *Carl Czerny: Über den richtigen Vortrag der sämtlichen beethoven'schen Klavierwerke.* Vienna: Universal Edition, 1963.

Czerny

Carl Czerny, "Recollections from My Life," translated by Ernest Sanders (from "Erinnerungen aus meinem Leben," 1842), *The Musical Quarterly*, XLII (1956), 302–17.

Frimmel/*Beethoven*

Theodor von Frimmel, *Beethoven-Studien*, 2 vols. (especially "Beethoven als Klavierspieler," II, 203–71). Munich: G. Müller, 1905, 1906.

Grundmann & Mies

Herbert Grundmann and Paul Mies, *Studien zum Klavierspiel Beethovens und seiner Zeitgenossen.* Bonn: H. Bouvier, 1966.

Huber/*Beethoven*

Anna Gertrud Huber, *Ludwig van Beethoven, seine Schüler und Interpreten.* Vienna: Krieg, 1953.

Kinsky & Halm/*Beethoven*

Georg Kinsky, *Das Werk Beethovens, thematisch-bibliographisches Verzeichnis seiner sämtlichen vollendeten Kompositionen*, completed by Hans Halm. Munich: G. Henle Verlag, 1955.

Kullak/*Beethoven*

Franz Kullak, *Beethoven's Piano Playing, With an Essay on the Execution of the Trill*, trans. by Theodore Baker (from the German preface to the Steingraber ed. of Beethoven's Piano Concertos, published in 1881). New York: G. Schirmer, 1901.

Newman/*Beethoven*

William S. Newman, *The Sonata Since Beethoven.* Chapel Hill: The University of North Carolina Press, 1969.

Newman/*Classic*

William S. Newman, *The Sonata in the Classic Era.* Chapel Hill: The University of North Carolina Press, 1963.

Chief References

Newman/*Cramer*

William S. Newman, "On the Rhythmic Significance of Beethoven's Annotations in Cramer's Etudes," scheduled for publication in the *Kongressbericht* of the International Musicological Society in Bonn, September 5–7, 1970.

Newman/*Liszt*

William S. Newman, "Liszt's Interpreting of Beethoven's Piano Sonatas," scheduled for publication in *Acta Musicologica* and the *Journal of the American Liszt Society* following the International Musicological Society Symposium on "Music in Europe During the Nineteenth Century," in Paris, September 1–5, 1970.

Newman/*Pianos*

William S. Newman, "Beethoven's Pianos Versus His Piano Ideals," *Journal of the American Musicological Society*, XXIII/3 (Fall, 1970), 484–504.

Newman/*106*

William S. Newman, "Some 19th-Century Consequences of Beethoven's 'Hammerklavier' Sonata, Op. 106," in *The Piano Quarterly*, No. 67 (Spring, 1969), 12–18, and No. 68 (Summer, 1969), 12–17.

Nottebohm/*Beethoveniana*

Gustav Nottebohm, *Beethoveniana: Aufsätze und Mittheilungen*. Leipzig: Peters, 1872.

Nottebohm/*Zweite*

Gustav Nottebohm, *Zweite Beethoveniana: nachgelassene Aufsätze*. Leipzig: Rieter-Biedermann, 1887.

Prod'homme/*Beethoven*

Jacques-Gabriel Prod'homme, *Les Sonates pour Piano de Beethoven*. Paris: Delagrave, 1937.

Rothschild/*Performance*

Fritz Rothschild, *Musical Performance in the Times of Mozart & Beethoven*. New York: Oxford University Press, 1961. (But see *The Piano Quarterly*, No. 36 [Summer 1961], 25–26 [William S. Newman]).

Schindler & MacArdle/*Beethoven*

Anton Felix Schindler, *Beethoven as I Knew Him*, translated by Constance S. Jolly and annotated by Donald W. MacArdle (from the 3rd ed. of 1860), 2 vols. in one. Chapel Hill: The University of North Carolina Press, 1966. Slight revisions have been made in some passages quoted in the present book.

Schenker & Ratz/*Beethoven*-m

Heinrich Schenker (ed.), *Beethoven: Klaviersonaten, nach den Autographen und Erstdrucken*, revised by Erwin Ratz, 4 vols. Vienna: Universal, 1946–47.

Schiedermair/*Beethoven*

Ludwig Schiedermair, *Der junge Beethoven*. Leipzig: Quelle & Meyer, 1925.

Tovey/*Beethoven*-m

Donald Francis Tovey (ed.), *Beethoven*:

Sonatas for Pianoforte, 3 vols. London: The Associated Board of the Royal Schools of Music [1931].

Wallner/*Beethoven*-m

Bertha A. Wallner (ed.) , *Beethoven: Klaviersonaten, nach Eigenschriften und Originalausgaben*, 2 vols. Munich: G. Henle, 1952–53, with minor revisions dated 1967. Examples quoted here include revisions for a further printing of this edition.

Wegeler & Ries/*Beethoven*

Franz Gerhard Wegeler and Ferdinand Ries, *Biographische Notizen über Beethoven*. Koblenz: K. Bädeker, 1838.

INDEX